# Revolving Funds and Business Enterprises of the Government, Exclusive of Lending Agencies

## A REPORT WITH RECOMMENDATIONS

PREPARED FOR

### THE COMMISSION ON ORGANIZATION OF THE

### EXECUTIVE BRANCH OF THE GOVERNMENT

*by*

Haskins & Sells, Certified Public Accountants, New York City, Under Direction of Maj. Gen. Arthur H. Carter, Former Fiscal Director, Army Service Forces; Col. Andrew Stewart, Former Deputy Director, Army Service Forces.

GREENWOOD PRESS, PUBLISHERS
WESTPORT, CONNECTICUT

Originally published in 1949
by the U.S. Government Printing Office, Washington, D.C.

First Greenwood Reprinting 1970

Library of Congress Catalogue Card Number 69-13926

SBN 8371-3168-5

Printed in the United States of America

# Letter of Transmittal

WASHINGTON, D. C.
*13, January, 1949.*

DEAR SIRS: In accordance with Public Law 162, approved July 7, 1947, the Commission on Organization of the Executive Branch of the Government has undertaken an examination into the operation and organization of the executive functions and activities. In this examination it has had the assistance of various task forces which have made studies of particular segments of the Government. Herewith, it submits to the Congress a study, prepared for the Commission's consideration on certain aspects of revolving funds and business enterprises of the Government other than lending agencies.

The study of each task force naturally is made from its own particular angle. The Commission, in working out a pattern for the Executive Branch as a whole, has not accepted all the recommendations of the task forces. Furthermore, the Commission, in its own series of reports, has not discussed all the recommendations of an administrative nature although they may be of importance to the officials concerned.

The Commission's own report in this particular field is submitted to the Congress separately.

The Commission wishes to express its appreciation to Haskins & Sells, Certified Public Accountants, New York City; to Maj. Gen. Arthur H. Carter, former fiscal director, Army Service Forces, and Col. Andrew Stewart, former deputy fiscal director, Army Service Forces, who prepared this task force study.

Faithfully,

*Chairman.*

*The Honorable*
   *The President of the Senate.*

*The Honorable*
   *The Speaker of The House of Representatives.*

# Contents

*III. Reports on Individual Government-Owned Hydroelectric, etc.—*Con.

*IV. Other Government Enterprises, Exclusive of Lending Agencies*

*V. Consideration of the Use of Revolving Funds*

*VI. The Use of the Corporate Form for Government Enterprises*

# SUMMARY REPORT

November 8, 1948.

Hon. Herbert Hoover,
*Chairman, Commission on Organization of the
Executive Branch of the Government,
Washington, D. C.*

Dear Sir: We submit the following as a summary of our report of November 3, 1948, for your convenience in studying our recommendations. This summary is subject to all of the qualifications which are contained in that report which was divided into six main sections as follows:

I. Government-owned hydroelectric projects.

II. The Reclamation Fund.

III. Reports on Individual Government-owned Hydroelectric Projects.

IV. Other Government enterprises, exclusive of lending agencies.

V. Consideration of the use of revolving funds.

VI. The use of the corporate form for Government enterprises.

The names of the Government projects and enterprises which we have surveyed are set forth in our report of November 3, 1948.

Our recommendations with respect to the first group (and where applicable to other Government enterprises) are summarized as follows:

1. That an intermediate screening board be established to (1) study the proposals for all power and reclamation projects; (2) review budget appropriation requests during periods of construction; (3) promulgate rules for the preparation of, and review of, allocations of costs, annual reports of operations, and repayment reports; and (4) make recommendations to the Congress based upon the board's studies of proposed projects and reviews of reports on existing projects.

2. That specifically as to Tennessee Valley Authority (1) the Congress reconsider the present repayment requirements; and (2) all new construction be authorized by the Congress except in case of unforseen emergencies, as to which a fund of $1,000,000 is available.

3. That the Reclamation Laws be codified and clarified.

4. That the Congress require the Bureau of Reclamation to furnish a complete and accurate report of the Reclamation Fund in all of its aspects.

5. That the authority of the General Accounting Office to make business-type audits of Government corporations be extended to all Bureau of Reclamation projects and all other power projects.

6. That the accounting systems and organization of the Bureau of Reclamation be revised.

7. That the functions and authority of the Federal Power Commission with respect to Government-owned hydroelectric projects be extended and made uniform.

8. That, wherever feasible, power produced at Government-owned hydroelectric projects be sold at the bus bar.

9. That the rates for the sale of electric energy generated at Government-owned hydroelectric projects be not considered as a "yardstick" for comparison with the rates charged by private industry.

10. That consideration be given to abolishing the Reclamation Fund.

11. That certain funds be transferred from the Reclamation Fund to the Treasury Department as miscellaneous receipts in accordance with legal requirements.

12. That, in general, the use of revolving funds for Government corporations and business-type enterprises (exclusive of lending agencies) be limited to funds for working capital.

13. That the corporate form be used for Government enterprises whose operations consist predominantly of business-type transactions with the public or with private industry and whose major programs are revenue producing.

14. That appropriations for construction costs and appropriations for operation and maintenance costs be made separately and be shown separately in all financial reports.

15. That borrowings by Government corporations and business-type agencies be made only from the Treasury Department or pursuant to approval by the Secretary of the Treasury.

16. That all appropriations which the Congress may determine to be repayable from revenue-producing operations bear interest.

17. That no Government agencies other than the Treasury Department be permitted to purchase Government securities.

Reasons for and discussion of these recommendations are presented with them in our principal report.

With respect to Part IV—Other Government enterprises, exclusive of lending agencies—we repeat the foregoing recommendations numbered 12, 13, 14, 15, 16, and 17 (which are of general application) and add the following recommendations with respect to certain of the enterprises:

2

As to the United States Maritime Commission, we recommend:

1. That the following recommendations made by the President's Advisory Committee on the Merchant Marine (K. T. Keller, Chairman) in its report of November 1947 be adopted:

*a.* That executive and operative functions now assigned to the Commission be vested in a single administrator who in time of peace would report to the Secretary of Commerce.

*b.* That a Maritime Board composed of the five commissioners exercise the quasi-legislative and quasi-judicial functions for which the Commission is presently responsible.

*c.* That a revolving fund of limited amount be restored, or a separate shipbuilding authorization with suitable contract authority be established, preferably the former.

*d.* That the present requirement of section 201 (b) of the Merchant Marine Act of 1936 be modified so as to require disassociation from the shipping industry on the part of a member of the Maritime Commission only during tenure of office rather than, as now, for 3 years prior to his appointment.

2. That the bad accounting situation described in our principal report [1] be left in the hands of the groups representing the Senate Committee on Expenditures in the Executive Departments and the General Accounting Office which are cooperating with the Maritime Commission.

As to Inland Waterways Corporation (and its wholly owned subsidiary, Warrior River Terminal Company), we recommend that action be taken on the recommendations already made by various individuals and committees, such as those contained in the audit report for the fiscal year ended June 30, 1946, prepared by the General Accounting Office, Corporation Audits Division, in the report of the Committee on Small Business in which it is recommended that the Government withdraw from the barge business, and the report of the Trundle Engineering Co.

As to Puerto Rico Reconstruction Administration and the Virgin Islands Company, special reports with recommendations have been made by representatives of the Department of the Interior and by a Congressional group, respectively.

In connection with all of the foregoing, reference is made to the portions of our principal report dated November 3, 1948, which deal individually with the above enterprises.

All of the enterprises which we have surveyed (except very recently the Maritime Commission) have been operated on a "revolving fund" basis, which is defined and discussed on pages 164 to 171, inclusive, of our principal report. Briefly, it may be said that the revolving-fund

---

[1] Since the date of our report on the Maritime Commission, August 17, 1948, we have noted that the Treasury Department, in its daily statement for October 15, 1948, omits all figures for the Maritime Commission and states in a footnote that publication of current data will be resumed when available.

operation involves the application of receipts from income or realization of assets as repayments to appropriations, thus making it possible to use the same fund over and over again for the authorized purpose.

These revolving-fund agencies are engaged in a variety of activities, some of which compete, at least in some degree, with private enterprise, and some of which do not. Some of them make payments to the States in which they operate in lieu of taxes, while others make no such payments; none of them make payments to the Federal Government equivalent to Federal taxes on similar privately owned enterprises. There are considerable variations in the accounting principles observed and in the manner in which the accounts have been maintained.

The "Government Corporations Control Act," approved December 6, 1945, provides, among other things, for the preparation of annual business-type budgets by each wholly owned Government corporation and for annual audits by the General Accounting Office in accordance with the principles and procedures applicable to commercial corporate transactions. Of the hydroelectric projects listed herein (group I), only Tennessee Valley Authority is affected (subject to certain reservations) by this act, which, as to part IV appears to be applicable to Panama Railroad Company, Federal Prison Industries, Inc., Inland Waterways Corporation (and its subsidiary), and the Virgin Islands Company. In this connection reference is made to our recommendations as summarized herein, numbered 5, 12, and 13.

In our surveys we have given no consideration to, and express no opinion regarding, questions of private versus Government enterprise. We are concerned solely with effective administration and believe that application of the following principles would be conducive thereto:

a. All revolving-fund agencies should be permitted the flexibility of private business concerns so far as consistent with the requisite checks and balances of the executive and legislative branches of the Government.

b. Commercial-type budgets of their operations (with appropriate distinction between capital and revenue items) should be prepared and submitted for the approval of the President and the Congress.

c. Adequate provision should be made for replacement and/or depreciation reserves.

As previously stated herein, we recommend that the corporate form be used for Government enterprises whose operations consist predominantly of business-type transactions with the public or with private industry and whose major programs are revenue-producing. As to such enterprises, we think incorporation should be under Federal

4

rather than State law and so far as practicable by uniform charter. The management of each such Government corporation should be vested in a small board of directors, acting on a part-time basis, who would be responsible, within the limits of authority prescribed by the Congress, for policy-making, including approval of condensed business-type budgets, and appointment of the principal officers. Such officers should include a comptroller capable of achieving the requisite cooperation with management at the top level and of giving adequate supervision to the accounts.

We include in this report as an appendix a draft of a proposed form of charter for Government corporations which has been prepared by John E. Masten and submitted to your Commission. We are, of course, not qualified to express an opinion as to the legal aspects of the proposed form of charter and there are certain of its provisions which seem to involve questions of national policy which we regard as beyond the sphere of our special qualifications as accountants. Such a provision is that in section 8 which would appear to make Government corporations subject to all taxes which are applicable to corporations organized under State laws. The proposed charter also contains provisions requiring that interest-bearing notes be given to the Treasury Department for advances received for capital and working funds. It seems to us that, while this requirement would serve no essential accounting purpose and would place some procedural burdens on those concerned, it no doubt would facilitate the carrying out of the will of the Congress in those cases where repayment is required of amounts expended pursuant to appropriation.

Yours truly,

HASKINS & SELLS.

# Proposed Form of Charter for Government Corporations

## AN ACT

creating the _____ Corporation

(NOTE.—The following proposed text is intended primarily to illustrate the recommendations to the Commission. It does not attempt to deal with all the matters of detail, or the variations in matters of policy, which may arise in connection with the creation of a particular Government corporation for a particular purpose.)

*Be it enacted by the Senate and House of Representatives of the United States of America in Congress assembled, as follows:*

SECTION 1. (a) There is hereby created a body corporate with the name _____ Corporation (hereinafter called the "Corporation") for the purpose of _____.

(b) The principal office of the Corporation shall be located in _____ _____. The Corporation may establish branch offices at such other places [1] in the United States as its Board of Directors shall deem necessary for the conduct of its business.

(c) The Corporation shall have succession through June 30, 19____, unless prior to that date it shall be dissolved by an Act of the Congress.

SEC. 2. Subject to the provisions of the Government Corporation Control Act, as amended, and the other provisions of this Act, the Corporation shall have power

(a) to adopt, alter and use a corporate seal;

(b) to adopt, amend and repeal bylaws, rules and regulations governing the conduct of its business;

(c) to purchase, lease or otherwise acquire, own, hold, maintain, use, operate, sell, lease or otherwise dispose of, property, real or personal, tangible or intangible;

(d) to accept gifts and contributions of services or property, real or personal, tangible or intangible, to aid it in carrying out its purposes under this Act;

(e) to make and perform contracts and agreements with any agency or instrumentality of the United States or any Territory, dependency or possession thereof, any State, any political subdivision of any of the foregoing, or any person, firm, association or corporation;

(f) without regard to the provisions of any of the Civil Service laws now or hereafter applicable to officers and employees of the United States, to select and employ officers, attorneys, agents and employees, to define their duties and establish a system of organization which shall fix their responsibilities and promote efficiency, to fix and pay their compensation, and to require bonds of any of them in its discretion and pay the premiums therefor;

(g) to determine the necessity for and the character and amount of its expenditures and the manner in which they shall be incurred, allowed, paid and accounted for, without regard to the provisions of any other laws governing the expenditure of public funds;

---

[1] If the principal office of the Corporation is located outside the District of Columbia, the act should require the establishment of a branch office there.

7

(h) to sue and be sued, to complain and to defend, in any court of competent jurisdiction, Federal, State or local; provided, that for the purposes of venue in civil actions the Corporation shall be deemed to be a resident of _____ _____; and

(i) to take all such actions as it shall deem necessary or appropriate in the exercise of the powers granted to it by this or any subsequent Act of the Congress.

Sec. 3. (a) Subject to the provisions of the Government Corporation Control Act, as amended, and the other provisions of this Act, the Corporation shall have power:

(1) to_____
_____;

(2) to_____
_____; and

(3) to_____
_____.

(b) The powers specified in subsection (a) of this Section 3 shall be subject to the following restrictions and limitations:

(1) _____
_____;

(2) _____
_____; and

(3) _____
_____.

Sec. 4. (a) The business of the Corporation shall be managed by a Board of Directors consisting of _____ persons appointed by the President of the United States with the advice and consent of the Senate. The Board shall have all the powers and authority granted to the Corporation under this and any subsequent Act of the Congress. After confirmation of the Directors by the Senate, the President shall designate one of them to serve as Chairman of the Board for a period coextensive with his term as Director. The Board of Directors shall meet for organization purposes upon call of the Chairman, who shall also call all subsequent meetings until by-laws governing its meetings shall have been adopted by the Board. Thereafter, all meetings of the Board shall be called and held as provided in the bylaws. A majority of the members of the Board shall constitute a quorum for the transaction of business.

(b) The members of the Board, each of whom shall be a citizen of the United States, shall be appointed upon the basis of proven ability, experience, reputation and standing, without regard for political affiliation or any other qualification of a political nature. Before entering upon the duties of his office, each Director shall take an oath to support the Constitution of the United States and to discharge faithfully and impartially the duties imposed upon him by this Act. The term of office of each Director shall be _____ years commencing the date of his appointment, provided, that the terms of office of the Directors first appointed shall be as follows: _____.[2] Upon the expiration of his term of office, a Director may continue in office until his successor is appointed and qualified. Directors shall be eligible for reappointment. Whenever a vacancy shall occur in an office of Director other than by expiration of term, the person appointed to fill such vacancy shall hold office for the unexpired

_____

[2] The term of office of a Director should not exceed 4 years. If the number of directors does not exceed four, the term of office of one of the Directors initially appointed should be 1 year, of the second 2 years, of the third 3 years, and of the fourth 4 years. If the number of Directors exceeds four, the term of office of the fifth Director initially appointed should be 1 year, of the sixth 2 years, etc.

8

portion of the term of his predecessor. Each Director, including the Chairman, shall receive a director's fee of $_____ for each meeting of the Board attended by him, and a per diem allowance of $_____ per day for time spent by him on special service for the Corporation at the request of the Board.

(c) The Board of Directors shall transmit to the Congress and to the President of the United States, semi-annually as of June 30 and December 31 of each year and within 90 days thereafter, a complete and detailed report of the operations of the Corporation during the 6 months next preceding the date thereof.

SEC. 5. (a) The Board of Directors shall select, appoint and fix the compensation of all officers of the Corporation, and such officers shall serve at the pleasure of the Board. The chief executive officer of the Corporation shall be its President, and the other officers of the Corporation shall consist of one or more Vice Presidents, a Secretary, a Treasurer, a Controller, a General Counsel and such subordinate officers as may be deemed necessary by the Board.

(b) In the appointment and promotion of all officers, attorneys, agents and employees of the Corporation, no political test or qualification shall be permitted or given consideration, but all such appointments and such promotions shall be given and made upon the basis of merit and efficiency. Any member of the Board who shall be found by the President of the United States to have violated the provisions of this subsection (b) shall be removed from office by the President forthwith, and any appointee of the Board who shall be found by the Board to have violated the provisions of this subsection (b) shall be removed from office by the Board forthwith.

(c) No director, officer, attorney, agent or employee of the Corporation shall participate in any manner, directly or indirectly, in the deliberation upon or the determination of any question by the Corporation affecting his personal interests or the interests of any corporation, partnership, or association in which he is directly or indirectly interested.

(d) All directors, officers, attorneys, agents, and employees of the Corporation shall be reimbursed by the Corporation for reasonable expenses, including travel and subsistence expenses, necessarily paid by them in the performance of their duties for the Corporation, without regard to the Subsistence Expense Act of 1926, as amended, or the Standardized Government Travel Regulations.

(e) No director, officer, attorney, agent, or employee of the Corporation shall be deemed to be an officer or employee of the United States for any purpose under any law of the United States.

SEC. 6. (Alternative No. 1.—For corporations such as the "lending agencies", which will incur few capital expenditures and in the case of which the segregation of funds for such expenditures from working capital is not a matter of importance.)

(a) The Corporation shall borrow all its capital funds from the Treasury of the United States, except as otherwise provided in subsection (c) of this section: *Provided,* That the aggregate amount of capital funds loaned by the Treasury to the Corporation shall not exceed $_____ outstanding at any one time. There is hereby authorized to be appropriated, out of any money in the Treasury not otherwise appropriated, the sum of $_____ for such loans. Such loans shall be evidenced by non-negotiable notes, payable to the Treasury, issued by the Corporation at such times and in such amounts, subject to the foregoing provisions, as its Board of Directors shall determine. Such notes shall mature not later than June 30, 19____,[3] shall be redeemable at any time prior to maturity at the option of the Corporation, and shall bear interest from their respective issue dates until paid at rates which shall be determined

[3] The date specified in sec. 1 (c).

annually by the Secretary of the Treasury upon the basis of the current average rate on outstanding marketable obligations of the United States. The Secretary of the Treasury is hereby authorized and directed to make such loans to the Corporation from funds appropriated therefor.

(b) The capital funds of the Corporation shall be kept at all times at the minimum consistent in the judgment of its Board of Directors with its requirements. The Board of Directors shall determine semianually whether its capital funds on hand exceed its requirements for the next succeeding semiannual period, and any excess capital funds so determined shall be applied forthwith by the Corporation to the prepayment of its outstanding notes issued under subsection (a) of this section: *Provided*, That the Treasury shall hold any funds so applied subject to further borrowing by the Corporation from time to time, without need for appropriations, in the manner provided in said subsection (a). After the payment in full of all outstanding notes of the Corporation, any excess funds so determined shall be paid forthwith by the Corporation into the Treasury of the United States as miscellaneous receipts, which shall not, be subject to further borrowing by the Corporation.

(c) If the operations of the Corporation on a cumulative basis from the effective date of this Act to the end of any fiscal year shall result in a deficit, its Board of Directors may recommend to the Congress that funds equal in amount to such deficit be appropriated for the Corporation. Such recommendation, with supporting data, shall be made in the budget program for the next succeeding fiscal year submitted by the Corporation pursuant to the Government Corporation Control Act, as amended. Any funds so appropriated, when received by the Corporation, shall be added to its funds on deposit with the Treasurer of the United States, and shall be credited on the books of the Corporation to a special "appropriation account to cover deficit."

(d) The Corporation shall not have any capital stock.

(*Alternative No. 2.*—For corporations which will make substantial expenditures, over a period of years, for revenue-producing facilities, and in the case of which the segregation of funds for such expeditures from working capital is desirable.)

(a) The Corporation shall borrow all its capital funds from the Treasury of the United States, except as otherwise provided in subsection (c) of this section; *Provided*, That the aggregate amount of capital funds loaned by the Treasury to the Corporation shall not exceed $_____ outstanding at any one time, of which not exceeding $ _____ shall be for capital expenditures and not exceeding $_____ for working capital. There is hereby authorized to be appropriated, out of any money in the Treasury not otherwise appropriated, the sum of $_____ for such loans. Each appropriation for such loans shall specify (1) the portion thereof which may be used for capital expenditures and the annual rate of repayment commencing 19____ of such portion according to a schedule of annual repayments which shall not be less than the straight-line depreciation provision applicable to the Corporation's physical properties determined in accordance with generally accepted accounting principles, and (2) the portion thereof which may be used for working capital. Such loans shall be evidenced by nonnegotiable notes, payable to the Treasury, issued by the Corporation at such times and in such amounts, subject to the foregoing provisions, as its Board of Directors shall determine. Notes evidencing loans for capital expenditures are hereinafter referred to as "capital notes" and the proceeds thereof as "capital funds," and notes evidencing loans for working capital are hereinafter referred to as "working capital notes" and the proceeds thereof as "working capital funds." All such notes shall mature not later than June 30, 19____,[4] shall be redeemable

---

[4] The date specified in sec. 1 (c).

at any time prior to maturity at the option of the Corporation, and shall bear interest from their respective issue dates until paid at rates which shall be determined annually by the Secretary of the Treasury upon the basis of the current average rate on outstanding marketable obligations of the United States. Capital notes shall mature serially in accordance with the rate of repayment specified in the appropriation authorizing the loans evidenced thereby. The Secretary of the Treasury is hereby authorized and directed to make such loans to the Corporation from funds appropriated therefor.

(b) The Corporation shall maintain separate accounts on its books for capital funds and working capital funds, and separate deposit accounts with the Treasury, and any other authorized depository, on the same basis. The capital funds and working capital funds of the Corporation shall be kept at all times at the minimum consistent in the judgment of its Board of Directors with its requirements. The Board of Directors shall determine semiannually whether its capital funds and working capital funds on hand exceed its requirements for the next succeeding semi-annual period, and any excess capital or working capital funds so determined shall be applied forthwith by the Corporation to the prepayment of its outstanding capital or working capital notes, respectively; *Provided*, That the Treasury shall hold any working capital funds so applied subject to further borrowing by the Corporation from time to time, without need for appropriations, in the manner provided in subsection (a) of this Section. After the payment in full of all outstanding working capital notes of the Corporation, any excess working capital funds so determined shall be applied forthwith by the Corporation to the prepayment of its outstanding capital notes. Any excess capital or working capital funds applied by the Corporation to the prepayment of its capital notes pursuant to this subsection (b) shall not be subject to further borrowing by the Corporation. After the payment in full of all outstanding capital notes of the Corporation, any excess capital or working capital funds so determined shall be paid forthwith by the Corporation into the Treasury of the United States as miscellaneous receipts, which shall not be subject to further borrowing by the Corporation.

(c) If the operations of the Corporation on a cumulative basis from the effective date of this Act to the end of any fiscal year shall result in a deficit, its Boards of Directors may recommend to the Congress that funds equal in amount to such deficit be appropriated for the Corporation. Such recommendation, with supporting data, shall be made in the budget program for the next succeeding year submitted by the Corporation pursuant to the Government Corporation Control Act, as amended. Any funds so appropriated, when received by the Corporation, shall be added to its working capital funds on deposit with the Treasurer of the United States, and shall be credited on its books to a special "appropriation account to cover deficit".

(d) The Corporation shall not have any capital stock.

Sec. 7. (a) The Corporation shall not expend any of its funds, regardless of source, for any purpose not authorized by section 2 and section 3 of this Act; *Provided*, That no expenditures for plant, plant expansion, or plant replacement (as distinguished from plant maintenance or repairs) shall be made by the Corporation unless specifically authorized by the Congress; and *provided, further*, That said section 2 and section 3 shall not be construed to authorize the Corporation to use any of its funds, regardless of source, for the purchase of obligations of, or guaranteed by, the United States.

(b) The Corporation shall not have any special privileges with respect to its use of the United States mails, but shall pay for such use at the applicable postal rates established by the Post Office Department.

(c) Debts due the Corporation shall not be entitled to the priority available to the United States under section 3466 of the Revised Statutes (31 U. S. C., Sec. 191).

(d) The Corporation shall not issue to the public, by sale or by any other method, any of its obligations in the form of bonds, notes, debentures or otherwise.

Sec. 8. The Corporation shall be subject to all taxes of every kind and description now or hereafter imposed by the United States, its territories, dependencies and possessions, and by any State, county, municipality or other local taxing authority upon corporations organized under State laws, but only to the same extent as such other corporations.

Sec. 9. (a) In the event of termination of the powers granted to the Corporation by section 3 of this Act prior to the expiration of its succession as provided in section 1 (c) hereof, its Board of Directors shall proceed forthwith to liquidate its assets and wind up its affairs. The Corporation may deposit with the Treasurer of the United States as a special fund any money belonging to the Corporation or from time to time received by it in the course of liquidation, for the payment of its outstanding obligations, which fund may be drawn upon or paid out for no other purpose. Any balance remaining after the liquidation of all the assets of the Corporation, and after provision has been made for payment in full of all its legal obligations other than its notes issued to the Secretary of the Treasury pursuant to subsection (a) of Section 6 hereof shall be used to pay such notes as shall then be outstanding. If such balance shall be more than sufficient to pay such outstanding notes in full, the excess shall be paid into the Treasury of the United States as miscellaneous receipts, and thereupon the Corporation shall automatically be dissolved. If such balance shall not be sufficient to pay such outstanding notes in full, an Act of the Congress shall be required to cancel such notes and dissolve the Corporation.

(b) If at the expiration of the succession of the Corporation, its Board of Directors shall not have completed the liquidation of its assets and the winding up of its affairs, the duty of completing such liquidation and such winding up shall be transferred to the Secretary of the Treasury, who, solely for such purpose and only to the extent necessary therefor, shall succeed to the powers and duties of the Board of Directors. In such event the Secretary of the Treasury may assign to any officer or officers of the United States in the Treasury Department the exercise and performance, under his general supervision and direction, of any of such powers and duties. When the Secretary of the Treasury shall determine that the continuance of such liquidation will no longer be advantageous to the United States and that adequate provision has been made for the payment in full of all of the legal obligations of the Corporation other than its notes issued to the Secretary of the Treasury pursuant to subsection (a) of section 6 hereof, he shall use any funds of the Corporation then remaining to pay such notes as shall then be outstanding. If such remaining funds shall be more than sufficient to pay such outstanding notes in full, the excess shall be paid into the Treasury of the United States as miscellaneous receipts, and thereupon the Corporation shall automatically be dissolved. If such remaining funds shall not be sufficient to pay such outstanding notes in full, an Act of the Congress shall be required to cancel such notes and dissolve the Corporation.

Sec. 11. Section 101 of the Government Corporation Control Act, as amended, is hereby amended by inserting therein, after the words "_____," the words "_____ Corporation."

Sec. 12. The right of the Congress to alter, amend or repeal this Act is hereby expressly reserved.

Sec. 13. If any provision of this Act or the application of such provision to any person or circumstances shall be held invalid, the validity of the remainder of this Act, and the applicability of such remainder to other persons or circumstances, shall not be affected thereby.

Sec. 14. This Act shall be known as the "_____ Corporation Act."

# INTRODUCTORY STATEMENT

NOVEMBER 3, 1948.

HON. HERBERT HOOVER,
*Chairman, Commission on Organization of the*
*Executive Branch of the Government,*
*Washington, D. C.*

DEAR SIR: In accordance with your instructions, we have made financial surveys of certain Government enterprises in order to assist you in carrying out the purposes of Public Law 162, Eightieth Congress, under which your Commission was appointed.

Our surveys have been based upon financial and other information available from official sources. We have regarded such information as reliable and have made no attempt to verify it through auditing procedures.

Moreover, we have not attempted to form a judgment with respect to the efficiency of the management of the enterprises or as to the wisdom of the national policies in relation thereto as prescribed by the Congress.

Our report consists of this introductory statement describing the scope of our work and stating our recommendations, and of the following six parts:

I. Government-owned hydroelectric projects.

II. The Reclamation Fund.

III. Reports on individual Government-owned hydroelectric projects.

IV. Other Government enterprises, exclusive of lending agencies.

V. Consideration of the use of revolving funds.

VI. The use of the corporate form for Government enterprises.

The enterprises included under I and IV above are as follows:

I. *Government-owned hydroelectric projects:*
　　Boulder Canyon—Hoover Dam.
　　Other Bureau of Reclamation Projects:

| | |
|---|---|
| Boise. | Rio Grande. |
| Minidoka. | Riverton. |
| Yakima. | Shoshone and Heart Mountain. |
| Central Valley. | Fort Peck. |
| Parker-Davis. | Colorado-Big Thompson. |
| Yuma. | Kendrick. |
| Grand Valley. | North Platte. |

I. *Government-owned hydroelectric projects*—Continued

    Columbia River Power System, consisting of Bonneville Dam Project, Columbia Basin Project—Grand Coulee Dam—and Bonneville Power Administration.

    Southwestern Power Administration.

    Tennessee Valley Authority.

IV. *Other Government enterprises, exclusive of lending agencies:*

United States Maritime Commission.

Rural Electrification Administration.

Panama Railroad Company.

Federal Prison Industries, Inc.

Inland Waterways Corporation and Warrior River Terminal Company.

Puerto Rico Reconstruction Administration.

The Virgin Islands Company.

Supplementing parts I and IV, we are including individual reports on the more important projects and on the other Government enterprises listed above and an appendix to part I showing examples of presentations and reports to which we have taken exception.

As is more explicitly pointed out later in this report, there are several matters with respect to which we are not qualified to, and do not, express an opinion. In particular, such subjects include the interpretation of legal and engineering matters.

We desire to make acknowledgment of the assistance received from the agencies concerned with the foregoing enterprises as well as from many other Government agencies and to state that all information requested was promptly furnished.

## Recommendations

Our recommendations, in the general order in which the subject matter is discussed herein, are as follows:

1. We recommend that an intermediate screening board be established to (1) study the proposals for all power and reclamation projects; (2) review budget appropriation requests during periods of construction; (3) promulgate rules for the preparation of, and review of, allocations of costs, annual reports of operations, and repayment reports; and (4) make recommendations to the Congress based upon the board's studies of proposed projects and reviews of reports on existing projects.

It seems doubtful whether the Congress, working through its appropriate committees, has available time adequately to review and study the enormous volume of written material regarding proposed power and reclamation projects [1] if, indeed, such committees have

---

[1] The size of the reports on the three principal basin developments is indicated by the following:

    Missouri Basin development, 211 pages of text.

    Colorado Basin development, 295 pages of text.

    Columbia Basin development, revised, 399 pages of text.

In each case, the text is accompanied by many maps, charts, etc.

available sufficient technical talent to arrive at a sound judgment. Consequently it seems to us that the studies and justifications prepared by the agencies which are to carry out the projects should not be used as a basis for legislative authorization of such projects without a prior complete and independent review, by a board of competent and technically qualified experts, as to the soundness and technical accuracy of such studies and justifications. The board should require all such proposals to be prepared on a consistent basis with standardized and simplified forms of project justification, and in conformity with whatever general rules of policy the Congress may decide upon; should ascertain that all subsidies are clearly indicated; and should eliminate duplicate or conflicting proposals by different agencies. The membership of the board should include persons with engineering and accounting qualifications and, because of the enormous expenditures involved, should include also a representative from the Council of Economic Advisers or from the Federal Reserve Board. The board could also be made responsible for reviewing budget appropriation requests during the construction periods to ascertain that all revisions of estimates necessary to bring the original justifications up to date are brought to the attention of the Congress. Furthermore, the board could aid the Congress by promulgating rules for the allocation of costs among the various purposes of the projects and for the preparation of operating and financial reports and repayment schedules of projects in operation, and by reviewing such allocations, reports, and schedules before they are presented to the Congress. This procedure should aid in eliminating many of the financial fallacies and inconsistent and misleading accounting practices referred to in greater detail in part I of this report and should result in furnishing the Congress with allocation reports, operating and financial reports, and repayment schedules which would be prepared on the same basis for all projects of like character and which would present the facts as to meeting repayment requirements, the true amounts of subsidies, etc., much more accurately and clearly than has been true in the past. If this plan were made effective, the clear, concise reports, already reviewed by a board directly responsible to the Congress, should make possible a considerable reduction in the time presently required to be spent by congressional committees.

2. We recommend specifically as to Tennessee Valley Authority (1) reconsideration by the Congress of the present repayment requirements and (2) that all new construction be authorized by the Congress except in case of unforeseen emergencies, as to which a fund of $1,000,000 is available.

While our computations indicate that the Authority is presently earning more than sufficient power revenues to repay the investment in power facilities, with interest, we recommend that the Congress reconsider the requirements for repayment as specified in the Government Corporations Appropriation Act of 1948 in view of the intent stated in the act "to make the power projects self-supporting and self-liquidating" and in particular that it determine (1) whether TVA should not pay into the Treasury all of its net income, or (2) whether the repayments should not be increased so as to be sufficient to repay the investment in 50 years with interest at 3 percent. In the latter case, while the amounts so required to be repaid would be almost double the present requirement, the earnings on the basis of 1947 results would be more than sufficient for that purpose. In either case, the computations of the amount to be repaid should provide for construction interest and also for interest on the unpaid balance of the debt allocable to completed power facilities.

All new construction should be authorized by the Congress, new appropriations being made therefor, and the Authority should not be permitted to construct new facilities with its power revenues, except in case of unforeseen emergencies as to which the fund of $1,000,000 is available and with respect to which subsequent approval could be obtained from the Congress.

3. We recommend that the reclamation laws be codified and clarified.

In our accompanying report on Government-owned hydroelectric projects, under the section "Legislation is Complicated and Indefinite," we point out some of the respects in which it is difficult, at least for a layman, to interpret the intent of Congress. Also, a great mass of separate laws (aggregating in excess of 800 pages) has accumulated over a period of many years, reflecting changes in reclamation policy arising from new conditions and new developments. It would seem that this would be an appropriate time to coordinate and simplify these laws, both in terms of general policy and of clearer and more detailed definitions of the various applications of that policy.

4. We recommend that the Congress require the Bureau of Reclamation to furnish a complete and accurate report of the reclamation fund in all of its aspects.

Reports prepared by the Bureau of Reclamation for the Congress are incomplete in many respects, and, in particular, fail to show cumulative totals, by sources, of all funds received and the disposition of those funds. In view of the large sums already appropriated to reclamation projects from general funds of the Treasury (which, under present law, will be repaid to the reclamation fund), and the vastly greater amounts that will be required if the proposed future programs are carried out, complete and accurate information on the source and use of these funds appears to be imperative. Such a report would be of great value to the Congress in the reexamination of reclamation policy recommended above. Further comments on the need for this

18

report are included in part I of this report, under the section entitled "The Reclamation Fund."

5. We recommend that the authority of the General Accounting Office to make business-type audits of Government corporations be extended to all Bureau of Reclamation projects and all other power projects.

Under the authority conferred by the Government Corporation Control Act, the General Accounting Office makes audits of all wholly owned Government corporations in accordance with principles and procedures applicable to commercial corporate transactions and under such rules and regulations as may be prescribed by the Comptroller General of the United States, and makes annual reports thereon to the Congress. These audits have proved to be an important and necessary means of control of the financial transactions of Government corporations. The only Government-owned hydroelectric project so audited is Tennessee Valley Authority, although Bonneville Power Administration is audited by independent public accountants. The Secretary of the Interior has recently requested that the General Accounting Office make business-type audits of all projects under the authority of the Bureau of Reclamation. We concur in this recommendation and recommend also that the necessary legislation be enacted to give the Comptroller General the same authority as he presently has with respect to Government corporations. We recommend, further, that this legislation specifically require the General Accounting Office to audit the reclamation fund and all other power projects. The magnitude of the operations of power and reclamation projects and of the reclamation fund is such that it is logical that the Congress should employ the same methods of control as are exercised with regard to wholly owned Government corporations, many of which, by comparison, are of lesser importance.

6. We recommend that the accounting systems and organization of the Bureau of Reclamation be revised.

The accounting systems employed in the Bureau of Reclamation and the lines of authority and responsibility are in need of revision. Several reports are prepared in different places covering the same subject matter and each set of figures is different in certain respects from the others. The principal difficulty seems to stem from a lack of definition of lines of accounting authority and lack of sufficient authority in the comptroller.

It is essential that the Comptroller of the Bureau of Reclamation, which carries on a business of great magnitude, should have complete authority over the accounts and should be responsible to the Commissioner of the Bureau, to the Secretary of the Interior, and to the Congress for all financial reports emanating from the Bureau.

We are informed that the General Accounting Office, the Treasury Department, and the Bureau of the Budget are engaged in a study, looking toward a major reorganization of the accounting of the Bureau. We accordingly recommend that this study be completed and that the necessary action be taken to correct the deficiencies noted above.

7. We recommend that the functions and authority of the Federal Power Commission with respect to Government-owned hydroelectric projects be extended and made uniform.

In order to correct the confused situation regarding the functions and authority of the Federal Power Commission with respect to Government-owned hydroelectric projects, as commented on in part I of this report, we recommend that legislation be enacted to give the Federal Power Commission authority in all Government-owned hydroelectric projects (*a*) to prescribe the system of accounts to be kept, (*b*) to approve all rate schedules for sale of electric energy and (*c*) to approve the annual provision for replacements and the balance in the reserve for replacements at the end of each year.

8. We recommend that, wherever feasible, power produced at Government-owned hydroelectric projects be sold at the bus bar.

In order to avoid unnecessary competition with private industry, and to reduce the use of public funds for the construction and operation of transmission facilities, all power generated at Government-owned hydroelectric plants should be sold at the bus bar (generating plant) unless, due to special circumstances, private industry is unable or unwilling to provide and operate such facilities. It is particularly important, in order to avoid economic waste as well as the unnecessary expenditure of Government funds, that there be no authorization for the construction of transmission lines which duplicate adequate privately owned lines already in existence.

9. We recommend that the rates for the sale of electric energy, generated at Government-owned hydroelectric projects be not considered as a "yardstick" for comparison with the rates charged by private industry.

Because of the many variations in the factors involved in the determination of rates for the sale of electric energy at Government-owned and privately owned power plants, we consider that there exists no fair basis of comparing the rates. Many of these factors are intangible. In this connection reference is made to part I of this report under the caption "Considerations Other Than Financial Results and Comparison of Government-owned With Privately Owned Projects."

10. We recommend that consideration be given to abolishing the Reclamation Fund.

Because the greater part of the funds for reclamation projects are now being appropriated from general funds of the Treasury, and for other reasons set forth in part I of this report under "The Reclamation Fund," the segregation of this fund no longer appears to serve any useful purpose. We therefore recommend that serious consideration be given to abolishing the fund.

11. We recommend that certain funds be transferred from the Reclamation Fund to the Treasury Department as miscellaneous receipts in accordance with legal requirements.

In some cases, reclamation projects have repaid to the reclamation fund the entire construction costs repayable from power revenues. and, pursuant to law, as set forth more fully in part I of this report under "Legislation is Complicated and Indefinite" subsequent power revenues from these projects should be covered into the Treasury as miscellaneous receipts. Insofar as we were able to determine, all such revenues have remained in the reclamation fund.

12. We recommend that, in general, the use of revolving funds for Government corporations and business-type enterprises (exclusive of lending agencies) be limited to funds for working capital.

Revolving funds, both for Government corporations and non-incorporated forms of Government enterprises (exclusive of lending agencies) should be permitted under conditions outlined in part V of this report under "Conclusions as to Revolving Funds." These conditions in general would limit the use of revolving funds to working capital with limited authority for temporary borrowing, net income to be paid into the Treasury monthly as miscellaneous receipts, and deficits to be reported to the Treasury currently and to the Congress at least once a year.

13. We recommend that the corporate form be used for Government enterprises whose operations consist predominantly of business-type transactions with the public or with private industry and whose major programs are revenue-producing.

The corporate form has certain advantages but should be used only where the proposed operations are predominantly of a business nature involving business-type transactions with the public or with private industry. At least the major programs should be revenue-producing. The management of such a corporation should be vested in a small board of directors on a part-time basis. For further details regarding this recommendation, see section VI of this report "The Use of the Corporate Form for Government Enterprises." Any business-type Government enterprise with respect to which this recommendation is not followed should, in any case, be brought under the provisions of the Government Corporation Control Act for a business-type audit by the General Accounting Office.

14. We recommend that appropriations for construction costs and appropriations for operation and maintenance costs be made separately and be shown separately in all financial reports.

In some instances, such as Bonneville Dam, combined appropriations have been made in the past for construction, operation, and maintenance. Also, in some financial reports all appropriations for construction, operation, and maintenance costs have been combined in one amount in the investment section of the balance sheet. Since appropriations for operation and maintenance costs are generally recovered currently through revenues, such appropriations should be shown separately from appropriations for construction costs (which represent the true investment), not only in the original appropriations and the annual financial reports, but also in all other statements, such as budgets, appropriation requests, etc.

In connection with the above, reference is made to alternate No. 2, Sec. 6 (a) of the proposed Government corporation charter, prepared by John E. Masten (p. 10).

15. We recommend that borrowings by Government corporations and business-type agencies be made only from the Treasury Department.

While, in certain instances in the past, borrowings from agencies of the Government other than the Treasury Department have been specifically permitted (as in the sale of bonds by TVA to the RFC) or specifically prohibited (as in Rural Electrification Administration), there appears to be no logical reason for permitting such borrowing, and we recommend the adoption of the general principle that borrowings by Government corporations and business-type agencies be made only from the Treasury Department or pursuant to approval by the Secretary of the Treasury.

16. We recommend that all appropriations which the Congress may determine to be repayable from revenue-producing operations bear interest.

At present, some enterprises pay interest on Government funds and others do not. Those which do not are, in effect, receiving a hidden subsidy in the amount of the interest. In order to put all enterprises on an equal basis in this respect, and to clearly reveal the amount of any such subsidy, interest on all expenditures under appropriations which are to be repaid from revenue-producing operations should be charged to the enterprise at rates to be fixed by the Secretary of the Treasury, presumably based on the average cost to the Treasury of borrowed money. We further recommend that the Congress include a provision to this effect in each such appropriation act.

17. We recommend that no Government agencies other than the Treasury Department be permitted to purchase Government securities.

There have been instances in which Government corporations have invested surplus funds in Government securities. However, this practice by Government corporations was prohibited (except under approval of the Secretary of the Treasury or with respect to amounts aggregating not more than $100,000 at any one time) by the "Government Corporations Control Act" (Public Law 248, 79th Cong., approved December 6, 1945). Apart from the fact that such transactions, if of substantial amount, might unduly influence the current operations of the Treasury Department, it is pointless for the Government to pay interest to itself. Accordingly, we recommend that the prohibition of this practice be extended to cover all Government agencies other than the Treasury Department. The payment into the Treasury by all Government corporations and business-type agencies of their net income (as recommended in item 12 above) would enable the Treasury to reduce the public debt pro tanto.

Yours truly,

HASKINS & SELLS.

# I. GOVERNMENT-OWNED HYDROELECTRIC PROJECTS

## Magnitude of Projects and Their Management

Government-owned hydroelectric and reclamation projects constitute a business of great magnitude. They are, in most cases, under the direction of the Bureau of Reclamation of the Department of the Interior, the principal exceptions being Tennessee Valley Authority which is a wholly owned Government corporation reporting directly to the President and the Congress, and certain dams operated by the Corps of Engineers, Department of the Army. A report rendered to your Commission by A. B. Roberts, consulting engineer, whose assistance in certain aspects of our work is acknowledged, shows that the total expenditures to date on such projects, including TVA and flood-control projects of the Corps of Engineers, plus the present estimated cost of those under construction or proposed, amount to over $40,-000,000,000, of which approximately one-half applies to projects of the Corps of Engineers. The total expenditures to June 30, 1947, on such projects were in excess of $2,000,000,000, and the costs proposed to be incurred thereafter amount to over $38,000,000,000.

Total personnel of the Bureau of Reclamation as of June 30, 1948, and of other power agencies as of January 1, 1948 (exclusive of certain personnel in the Department of the Interior who furnish administrative and supervisory service to the Bureau of Reclamation and exclusive of Corps of Engineers personnel engaged in construction and operation of power projects) was reported as follows:

| | |
|---|---|
| Bureau of Reclamation | 17, 035 |
| Tennessee Valley Authority | 14, 222 |
| Bonneville Power Administration | 1, 412 |
| Southwestern Power Administration | 72 |
| Total | 32. 741 |

The Corps of Engineers has constructed and now operates certain dams where an agency of the Department of the Interior is responsible for the transmission and sale of power generated thereat, e. g., Bonneville Dam and Denison and Norfork Dams (Southwestern Power Administration). The operation of the Grand Coulee Dam is under the Bureau of Reclamation, whereas Bonneville Power Administration, which distributes and sells power both at Bonneville and Grand Coulee Dams, reports directly to the Secretary of the Interior.

The above-mentioned report of A. B. Roberts cites evidence of competition and duplication between the Bureau of Reclamation and the Corps of Engineers in the proposed development of projects.

## Matters on Which We Express No Opinion

There are several matters to be considered in connection with the projects with respect to which we are not qualified to, and do not, express an opinion. Such matters include the interpretation of the legal meaning and the intent of enactments by the Congress, legal opinions thereon, Executive orders issued thereunder, and memorandums of understanding between two or more agencies regarding their respective functions. Further, we are not qualified to pass upon the propriety of the allocations of costs of the projects among power, irrigation, flood control, navigation, etc.

## Legislation Is Complicated and Indefinite

The reclamation laws are voluminous and complex, there being over 803 pages of laws which govern the operation of the Bureau of Reclamation. The legislation under which other power projects have been authorized is likewise complicated and shows a lack of uniformity. Some were authorized by special legislation, e. g., Hoover Dam and Bonneville Power Administration. Others were authorized under the provisions of the Reclamation Project Act of 1939 and the Flood Control Act of 1944, and the Tennessee Valley Authority was constiuted a Government corporation under special legislation. The separate enactments authorizing these projects contain varying provisions as to the fixing of rates for power and as to repayment requirements. Furthermore, the provisions of the Reclamation Project Act of 1939 seem to be indefinite in some respects and have been the subject of legal interpretations which to the lay mind seem to have added confusion to a muddled situation. Without invading the area of legal opinion, it is pertinent to point out some of the respects in which the law is confusing to a layman.

In section 9 (a) of the Reclamation Project Act of 1939, the Secretary is required to make an investigation and submit to the President and to the Congress his report and findings on:

1. The engineering feasibility of the proposed construction;

2. The estimated cost of the proposed construction;

3. The part of the estimated cost which can properly be allocated to irrigation and probably be repaid by the water users;

26

4. The part of the estimated cost which can properly be allocated to power and probably be returned to the United States in net power revenues;[2]

5. The part of the estimated cost which can properly be allocated to municipal water supply or other miscellaneous purposes and probably be returned to the United States.

Section 9 (c) requires the fixing of rates which, in the judgment of the Secretary, will produce "power revenues at least sufficient to cover an appropriate share of the annual operation and maintenance cost, interest on an appropriate share of the construction investment at not less than 3 percent per annum and such other fixed charges as the Secretary deems proper." A layman's construction of the foregoing would be that the cost allocated to power would be recovered with 3-percent interest. However, it has not been so interpreted by the Bureau of Reclamation. While allowance for interest at 3 percent has apparently been included in the rate structure, the interest computed on the unpaid balance of construction costs allocated to power is, in most instances, applied in the repayment schedules to the repayment of costs allocated to irrigation to be repaid by power revenues. There also seems to be confusion between two types of allocations of costs: (1) Allocations of costs to the purposes for which the project is authorized and (2) allocations of costs by the purposes from which repayment is expected. For example, section 9 (a) of this act, by failing to distinguish between allocations of cost to irrigation, power, and municipal water supply or other miscellaneous purposes, on one hand, and, on the other, the estimated cost which can probably be repaid or returned to the United States (repayable and returnable allocations), implies that the cost allocated to each purpose is the same as the cost which can probably be repaid or returned by that purpose. However, in most projects, feasibility has been determined by finding that a portion of the costs allocated to irrigation will be repaid from power revenues, as, in the case of the Columbia Basin project, where feasibility was determined on the basis that power revenues would repay, in addition to costs allocated to power, all joint costs allocated to irrigation (approximately $65,000,000) and approximately 65 percent of the cost of irrigation works (at 1945 prices the total cost of irrigation works was estimated at $355,344,000).

As to the disposition of moneys received in connection with projects, there are varying provisions:

1. All receipts from the Boulder Canyon project are to be paid into the Colorado River dam fund out of which repayment of advances for construction of the project is to be made to the Treasury with interest.

2. The Bonneville Project Act of 1937 provides that all receipts from the sale of energy generated at Bonneville Dam are to be covered into the Treasury as miscellaneous receipts.

---

[2] Par. (4) above should be particularly noted as requiring a determination of the part of the costs which can properly be allocated to power and probably be returned in net power revenues.

3. A provision similar to (2) above is included in the Flood Control Act of 1944 in connection with energy generated at projects under the control of the War Department.

4. The Interior Department Appropriation Act of 1939 contained a provision, known as the "Hayden-O'Mahoney amendment" that all revenues (including power revenues) of irrigation projects constructed by the Bureau of Reclamation shall be covered into the reclamation fund, except where, by law or contract, such revenues are to be used for the benefit of water users; provided, that after net revenues from the sale of power have repaid construction costs of a project allocated to power to be repaid by power revenues therefrom, further net power revenues shall be covered into the Treasury as miscellaneous receipts.

Though the repayment reports of the Bureau of Reclamation indicate that, for several projects, the construction costs to be repaid from power revenues have been fully repaid, the Treasury Department has not been requested to transfer, and has not transferred, any such power revenues from the reclamation fund to miscellaneous receipts. It should also be noted that the Hayden-O'Mahoney amendment in effect gives to the reclamation fund a subsidy for the benefit of reclamation projects of all moneys heretofore or hereafter appropriated by the Federal Government out of general funds for the construction of reclamation projects. As of June 30, 1947, the amounts so appropriated aggregated nearly $1,000,000,000, which, with interest at 3 percent during repayment periods of 50 years, would constitute a subsidy of almost double that amount if all repayments are appropriated for reclamation purposes.

## Lack of Uniformity in Legislation as to Approval of (a) Allocations of Costs, (b) Power Rates, and (c) Accounting

The lack of uniformity in legislation relating to Government-owned hydroelectric projects, referred to above, is further exemplified in a review of the extent to which the Federal Power Commission has authority over such projects.

The Federal Power Commission has no authority over Bureau of Reclamation projects. However, it has been given specific and varying authorities over certain projects, as shown by the following:

1. *Tennessee Valley Authority*

TVA is required to keep its accounts in accordance with the uniform system of accounts prescribed by the Federal Power Commission, and to render reports to the Commission.

2. *Bonneville project*

Under the Bonneville Act, the Federal Power Commission is given the following unusual powers: (a) To allocate costs to the various purposes, (b) to approve schedules of rates for electric energy, (c) to see that the accounts are

28

kept in accordance with the Federal Water Power Act, and (d) to designated a member of the advisory board on power.

It should be noted that the Federal Power Commission has no such jurisdiction over Grand Coulee Dam.

### 3. *Fort Peck project*

Under the Fort Peck Act, the Commission has the following powers: (*a*) To make an allocation of costs to various purposes, (*b*) to approve schedules of rates for electric energy, and (*c*) to see that the accounts are kept in accordance with the Federal Water Power Act.

### 4. *Projects Under Control of the Department of the Army, the Power From Which Is Sold by the Secretary of the Interior*

The Federal Power Commission is required to approve rates for power. It apparently also has some jurisdiction over allocations of costs to purposes, based on the following sentence in section 5 of the Flood Control Act of 1944:

"Rate schedules shall be drawn having regard to the recovery (upon the basis of the application of such rate schedules to the capacity of the electric facilities of the projects) of the cost of producing and transmitting such electric energy including the amortization of the capital investment allocated to power over a reasonable period of years."

While the act does not fix the responsibility for making allocations of costs, it would seem that it was intended that the Federal Power Commission should have some authority through its powers to approve rates.

It should be noted that the Federal Power Commission is not given authority to fix or approve the provisions for replacements, which is an important element in determining the net income of a project.

We are accordingly recommending that legislation be enacted to give the Federal Power Commission authority in all Government-owned hydroelectric projects (*a*) to prescribe the system of accounts, (*b*) to approve rate schedules, (*c*) to approve the annual provision for replacements and the total reserve at the end of the year, and (*d*) to make all allocations of costs between the various purposes of the project.

## Scope of Our Studies Defined

In view of the conditions described, the purposes of your Commission, and your instructions to us, we concluded that the most useful purpose we could serve would be to make financial surveys of existing financial data, and, in our role as public accountants, to consider the financial reports of the projects assigned to us in the light of our professional experience and to interpret such reports so as to present the facts as we see them. We saw no necessity for examining the authenticity of the financial statements, such as by the application of auditing procedures, and therefore confined our studies to existing data mostly in the form of public information supplemented, where required, by additional explanations obtained from the Government

**29**

agencies concerned. In other words, we have accepted the basic data as published by the various agencies, but have arrived at our own conclusions as to the proper interpretation thereof.

As to Bureau of Reclamation projects, the information on which our studies were based was obtained from reports of financial operations of Bureau of Reclamation power systems, repayment schedules and studies for power systems, project financial statements as of June 30, 1947, statements of power operations, digests of appropriations, and hearings on Interior Department appropriation bills. Limitations of time precluded a complete study of all available information, which is exceedingly voluminous. (For example, the hearings of the subcommittee of the Appropriations Committee of the House of Representatives on the 1949 Interior Department appropriation bill, covering only the Bureau of Reclamation, consist of over 2,400 pages.) As to other projects, we have reviewed the published annual reports and repayment schedules, where available, and have obtained additional data from the agencies concerned.

## Allocations of Costs Objected To

While, as stated, we are not qualified to pass upon the propriety of the allocations of costs among the several purposes of projects, there is considerable evidence in the record of objections to some of the allocations as being improper. For example, the recommendations of the General Accounting Office on the Tennessee Valley Authority, as included in the House hearings on the Government corporations appropriation bill for 1949, indicate that insufficient costs may have been allocated to power and that a new determination of the allocation of the cost of multiple-use facilities is needed as evidenced by the following extract from the recommendations:

On the basis of our review of the Authority's evaluation of the navigation and flood-control tangible benefits, the portion of the cost of multiple-use facilities allocated by the Board to the two purposes is not justified.

The Department of Agriculture and the Corps of Engineers have also criticized allocations made by the Bureau of Reclamation.

The importance of the propriety of the cost allocations should not be overlooked. Costs allocated to certain purposes are regarded as nonreimbursable; such purposes include flood control and navigation. The effect of allocating a portion of the cost of a project to such nonreimbursable purposes is to grant a subsidy to the residents of a particular area to be paid for by all taxpayers of the Nation. The greater the proportion of the costs charged to nonreimbursable purposes the greater is the subsidy and the more readily provable is the requisite economic feasibility. Another type of subsidy at the expense of all of the taxpayers is granted to the power and irrigation customers of reclamation projects to the extent that power revenues and construction charges assumed by water users do not repay the investment with interest. That portion of this latter subsidy which represents interest on irrigation costs to be repaid by water users has been recognized by the Congress under long-established law. However, there appears to be no specific congressional recognition of the subsidy represented by interest on power and irrigation construction costs to be repaid from power revenues. It is doubtful if these facts are sufficiently comprehended. Reference to subsidies is not complete without mentioning the contributions from general funds to the reclamation fund of nearly $1,000,000,000 referred to above.

## STANDARDS OF REPORTING

In a field of such magnitude from the financial viewpoint, and particularly where the applicable legislation is so complicated, it would seem that the minimum standard for presentation of financial data in relation to the projects involved should be one of complete disclosure of all relevant facts. Any failure to meet this standard is tantamount to misrepresentation to the Congress and to the public. In the light of what follows in this report, it may fairly be asked whether the Congress generally, or even the committees which have given a great deal of attention to these matters, are, or have been in a position to become, fully aware of the present situation.

Before presenting our criticisms of present financial and accounting practices, we wish to state that all of the officials of the Bureau of Reclamation and of other agencies with whom we have come in contact impressed us favorably. We realize that they have a difficult task to carry out the intent of a complicated set of laws and that certain practices which have been in force over a long period seem to have the force of law to those in charge of administration. We also wish to repeat that all information which we requested was promptly furnished. However, certain practices, though supported by legal opinion, are nonetheless financial fallacies in our opinion.

## FINANCIAL FALLACIES

Many of the financial presentations do not tell the full story, are complicated and inconsistent, and in some respects would seem to a layman to be contrary to the intent of Congress. This situation arises in part from certain financial fallacies which are apparently accepted doctrine in the Bureau of Reclamation. Some of these are:

1. That interest repays capital investment.

This is shown in practically all Bureau of Reclamation repayment schedules and is based in part on an opinion of a solicitor of the Department of the Interior (the Fowler Harper opinion referred to later in greater detail).

2. That because power rates include a charge for interest and because all revenues are deposited with the Treasury, the Treasury thereby receives interest on all projects.

In determining the rate structure, no consideration is given to recovering the costs of irrigation facilities to be repaid by power revenues (except to the extent that such costs may exceed interest on the construction costs allocated to power). The fallacy, therefore, is that, while an item called interest is included in the rate structure, a portion of the construction costs to be repaid by power is omitted and a rate so determined will not liquidate the project within a reasonable time. As indicated in (1) above, the interest on the unpaid balance of construction costs allocated to power is actually applied toward repayment of irrigation costs allocated to power for repayment. Except for the Grand Coulee Dam, as to which interest is paid to the Treasury as a separate item but is transferred to the reclamation fund, the Treasury has no means of distinguishing interest from principal in the deposits of gross revenues and, in fact, does not know whether or not the amounts deposited are sufficient to cover interest.

3. That interest during construction need not be included as part of the project cost. This is based on the Fowler Harper opinion with regard to the Columbia Basin project (Grand Coulee Dam) which also held that the interest component in the rate schedule need not be calculated from the time of actual expenditure and construction but from an "appropriate" later date.

In our opinion interest during construction is a proper element of cost and, if not included therein, the basis for repayment will be erroneous.

4. The voluminous reports on the Colorado, Missouri, and Columbia River basin-wide projects, which are intended as a justification for the authorization of the expenditure of large sums, are so prepared that they are likely to be misunderstood. In each of these official reports the impression is given that the projects are to pay interest at 3 percent and to amortize the investment within 50 years. A study of the justification demonstrates, however, that it is not the intention to make provision for interest. More detailed comments on these reports are included in the appendix to part I of this report (p. 98).

At this point it is appropriate to refer also to an anomaly, if not a fallacy, in the interpretation of section 14 of the Tennessee Valley Authority Act, which declares it to be the policy of the act that the

32

power project be self-supporting and self-liquidating. It appears to us that this can only mean that the project should repay the principal within a reasonable term of years together with a reasonable rate of interest. This was apparently the view of David E. Lilienthal, as a director, when he announced the original power rates. It was apparently also the view of Senator Homer Ferguson, as expressed in hearings before the Senate Committee on Appropriations, in April 1947. Nevertheless, the present chairman, Gordon R. Clapp, took the position at these hearings that the investment in TVA by the Government is like a common-stock equity, and that the use of the word "interest" is therefore avoided. Further reference to this matter is made in the appendix.

## Inconsistent or Misleading Accounting Practices

There is also evidence of inconsistent or misleading accounting practices, a few of which are mentioned here. Further details are given in the accompanying reports on the individual projects and in the appendix, which also includes extracts from congressional hearings.

In the course of reviewing the operations of the various power projects to June 30, 1947, and the projected future operations, several examples of inconsistent or misleading presentations were noted in the annual reports and repayment reports prepared by the various agencies and in the schedules prepared for congressional hearings. These are covered more specifically in our comments on the individual projects, but they include:

1. Exclusion of construction interest from financial statements of some projects and not from others.

2. Application of interest on investment allocated to power to the repayment of other costs to be repaid by power as to some Bureau of Reclamation projects and not as to others.

3. Different investment or earnings amounts shown by Bureau of Reclamation financial statements, repayment reports, and schedules included in congressional hearings.

4. Deduction of operating costs other than for power from power revenues of a project in the repayment report but not in the financial statements.

5. Including operating costs in repayment of Federal investment and the appropriations therefor in gross Federal investment in the balance sheet of a project and excluding from the Federal investment the cost of facilities allocated to irrigation to be repaid from power revenues, thereby implying a greater rate of repayment than actually exists with respect to the investment in facilities. More detailed reference to this matter is made later in this report.

6. Failure to revise repayment reports for increases in estimated total construction costs due to increases in the price level.

7. The requirements for the fixing of rates for power vary among the different projects.

8. The periods within which the costs of projects are to be amortized are not uniform. Hoover Dam and Bonneville Dam have 50-year repayment requirements. The Reclamation Project Act contains no provision fixing the amortization period, and various periods are used in the repayment reports.

9. By reason of defective methods employed in preparing repayment schedules and justifications, as referred to in the appendix and elsewhere in this report, the true amounts of subsidies involved are not disclosed.

## Rules for Determining Whether Projects Are Self-Sustaining and Self-Liquidating

In this area of varying requirements and interpretations, and confronted by official statements on the record that all power projects will repay every dollar of investment with interest, we concluded that our financial surveys of these projects would be of maximum value to your Commission if we applied to them a uniform set of rules, where feasible, to determine whether the projects are in fact self-sustaining and self-liquidating, using in each case the available facts and figures. By so doing we do not take the position that the amortization and interest method used is required by law or by any interpretative opinion thereof. Nor do we imply that by so doing we have correctly interpreted the intent of the Congress. However, the application of a uniform set of rules furnishes a basis for comparison of the projects and may also afford a basis for additional clarifying legislation where necessary.

As has been stated, all of our computations are based upon information furnished to us, which we have treated as reliable, including the allocations of costs to power, irrigation, flood control, navigation, and other purposes.

The investments allocated to power have been assumed to be repayable in equal annual installments of principal and interest within 50 years from the date at which each unit came into operation, with interest at 3 percent per annum compounded annually (except in the cases of the Columbia River power system where the rate of $2\frac{1}{2}$ percent fixed by the Federal Power Commission order allocating the costs of the Bonneville project has been applied to the operations of the entire Columbia River power system in their annual financial statements and the Southwestern Power Administration where the rate of $2\frac{1}{2}$ percent has also been assumed to be applicable). That part of the investment which is allocated to irrigation, and which will not be recovered through charges to water users but which has to be recovered from power revenues, is likewise treated as interest bearing and amortizable on the same basis as previously described. Thus,

34

ability to repay Federal investment is to be tested by comparing (a) net income from the project after provision for interim replacements and such payments in lieu of taxes as may be required by law but before deducting interest on the Federal investment, with (b) the annual payment which, on an equal-annual-payment basis, will amortize the investment repayable from power revenues within 50 years and also provide for interest at the specified rate.

There are minor variations in the application of the foregoing general rules but the effect of such variations is not considered significant.

### Reasons for Methods Used

It is a well-established practice in the Bureau of Reclamation to present justifications and repayment schedules which give the impression that the income from the project will be sufficient to repay the indebtedness in 50 years with 3 percent interest; in other words, that the project is self-sustaining and self-liquidating.

In studies of proposed projects which are submitted to the Congress for authorization, such as the Missouri River Basin project, the Columbia River Basin project, and the Colorado River Basin project, there is included in annual costs a provision for amortization of the investment within 50 years with interest at 3 percent compounded annually, although in the subsequent comparison of revenues with cost, interest is disregarded.

In the repayment studies prepared by the Bureau of Reclamation, the power rates provide net revenues in excess of 3 percent interest per annum on the original investment allocated to power. Interest on the unpaid balance of the investment allocated to power is shown later in a separate column under the title "Interest at 3 percent," although, by the subsequent application of this interest item in reduction of irrigation costs, the apparent provision of interest is nullified.

The Boulder Canyon project (Hoover Dam) was the largest of the earlier projects, having been approved by act of Congress dated December 21, 1928. The original act provided that before any money was appropriated for construction, the Secretary of the Interior should make provision for revenues by contract, adequate in his judgment to insure payment of all expenses of operation and maintenance and the repayment, within 50 years from the date of completion, of all amounts advanced, together with interest thereon. The original act provided for interest at 4 percent, but this was amended by the Adjustment Act of July 1940 to provide for interest at 3 percent compounded annually.

In the repayment schedule for Grand Coulee Dam, the Bureau of Reclamation makes provision for interest at 3 percent per annum on

**35**

the investment in facilities allocated to power with amortization over a 50-year period. In the Bonneville Power Administration financial statements, interest is provided at 2½ percent on the net investment allocated to power, for the reason that this rate of interest was determined by the Federal Power Commission in its allocation of costs for Bonneville Dam.

The Reclamation Project Act of 1939 provided that the rates for the sale of electric power should be at least sufficient to cover an appropriate share of the annual operation and maintenance cost, interest on an appropriate share of the construction investment at not less than 3 percent per annum, and such other fixed charges as the Secretary of the Interior deems proper. However, an opinion of a solicitor of the Department of the Interior (the Fowler Harper opinion) apparently nullifies the interest requirement by stating in effect that, if the repayments, consisting of interest at 3 percent per annum on the gross investment allocated to power, are equal to the construction costs to be repaid by power, no amount needs to be included in the rate structure for amortization of the construction costs; in other words, that the Reclamation Project Act permits, in such circumstances, a subsidy to the power consumers of the total construction cost and to the irrigator of the total cost allocated to irrigation to be repaid by power plus interest thereon.

With reference to the solicitor's opinion mentioned above, Congressman Jensen (Iowa), in hearings before the subcommittee of the Committee on Appropriations, House of Representatives, Eightieth Congress, second session, on the Interior Department appropriation bill for 1949, in referring to the transfer into the reclamation fund of interest paid on construction costs from the power revenues of Grand Coulee Dam, made the following statement:

And we are now by that very act complying with the basic law of the land which Mr. Fowler Harper, by one stroke of the pen, nullified, and which has caused no end of controversy and, in my estimation, has been very detrimental to reclamation, hydroelectric power funds, and everything else pertaining to reclamation, irrigation, and hydroelectric power projects.

Section 5 of the Flood Control Act of 1944 provides in effect that the rates for electric energy generated at projects under the control of the War Department shall be sufficient to recover the cost of producing and transmitting such energy "including the amortization of the capital investment allocated to power over a reasonable period of years."

The Tennessee Valley Authority Act provided in effect that the power projects thereof should be self-supporting and self-liquidating and, as already mentioned, this concept was interpreted in published announcements of the original power rates to require repayment of construction costs with interest. This interpretation is referred to again in the appendix.

36

TVA has not made provision on its books for interest on the investment of the United States Government in power facilities and it has been repeatedly pointed out in congressional hearings that, if the project is not chargeable with interest, there is a discrimination against the populations of other areas where Government-owned power projects are charged with interest and also against all other taxpayers of the Nation.

In view of the foregoing, the method of testing the ability of power projects to repay by applying uniformly a 50-year, equal-annual-payment plan including interest at 3 percent, compounded annually, in our opinion is fair and reasonable. However, our use of this basis is not to be construed as implying that there is a legal requirement to this effect.

We have given consideration to other methods under which annual payments would increase or decrease from year to year, but in view of the fact that power revenues tend to become stabilized soon after the facilities are put in service, we have selected the equal-annual-payment method.

Under this method, the annual payment required to amortize $100 of investment over a period of 50 years, with interest at 3 percent, compounded annually, is $3.88655. Thus, in a 50-year period, revenues required to retire $100 of investment would amount to 50 times $3.88655, or $194.33.

## PROVISION FOR REPLACEMENTS

In our study of the operating results of projects, we have been guided by the recommendations of the Federal Power Commission, in its Administrative Memorandum No. 12, that provisions for interim replacements in a Government-owned hydroelectic project should be 0.6 percent for generating plant and 0.9 percent for transmission plant, with $2\frac{1}{2}$ percent interest on the accumulative provision in each case. Where adjustment of the provision for replacements, as shown by financial reports of the projects, to the basis recommended by the Federal Power Commission would not have made any material difference in our conclusions, no adjustment has been made.

Since a 50-year equal-annual-payment plan with interest is being applied as a test of ability to repay the investment, it is not necessary to provide for depreciation but only for "interim replacements" (i. e., those which may reasonably be expected to be necessary in the 50-year period) as recommended by the Federal Power Commission. Accordingly in our studies, wherever provisions have been made for depreciation, we have added them back to income and have deducted from income provisions for replacements at the rates recommended by the Federal Power Commission. In the case of Tennessee Valley Authority the amount of depreciation provisions so restored to income was approximately $62,000,000 as compared with approximately $17,000,000 deducted from income for interim replacements.

### Provision for Interest During Construction

As previously mentioned herein (p. 33), interest on construction has been included in the official financial statements of some projects and excluded from those of others. As to those from which it has been excluded, we have, for comparative purposes, included such interest at computed amounts, in certain instances as set forth in the separate reports which follow on the Boulder Canyon, Colorado-Big Thompson, Southwestern Power Administration, and Tennessee Valley Authority projects. As to other projects, generally though not always where inclusion would have occasioned only unimportant changes in the indicated financial results, we have not revised the figures obtained from official sources, but have merely referred to the omission of interest during construction. This has been done in the cases of the Columbia Basin (Grand Coulee Dam) and Central Valley projects.

## Summaries of Results of Our Tests of Ability to Repay Investments

We summarize hereunder the results of our tests of ability to repay investments. Further details of such tests are submitted as to some of the projects in individual reports which follow this section.

In these tests, we have accepted, without question, the allocations of construction costs to reimbursable and nonreimbursable purposes. Reimbursable construction costs generally include costs allocated to power and irrigation and, in all cases, we have assumed that all irrigation construction costs in excess of anticipated payments by water users have been allocated to power for repayment purposes.

In the computations of net revenues, no amount is included as a charge against revenues for Federal, State, and local taxes, which would be payable if the project were owned by private interests instead of by the Federal Government. However, the Boulder Canyon project (Hoover Dam) makes annual payments to the States of Arizona and Nevada and the Colorado River development fund aggregating $1,100,000, which are regarded as payments in lieu of taxes; and TVA is required to make payments in lieu of taxes to State and local governments at rates gradually decreasing from 10 percent (in the fiscal year beginning July 1, 1940) to 5 percent (in the fiscal year beginning July 1, 1948, and thereafter) of the gross revenues from the sale of power to customers other than agencies of the Federal Government. The Federal Power Commission has reported for the year 1946 that Federal, State, and local taxes for all class A and B utilities in the United States averaged 19 percent of gross revenues or 5 percent of gross plant investment.

## BOULDER CANYON PROJECT—HOOVER DAM

Hoover Dam and the All-American Canal were authorized in 1928, and construction of the dam was begun in 1931 and completed in 1936. The legislation provided that advances by the Treasury for construction of the dam and power plant, exclusive of $25,000,000 allocated to flood control, were to be repaid in 50 years, with interest at 4 percent per annum and that power rates were to be determined on a competitive basis. The Boulder Canyon Project Adjustment Act reduced power rates by requiring that they be sufficient only to make annual payments to the States of Arizona and Nevada and the Colorado River development fund totaling $1,100,000 and to repay the advances, exclusive of the $25,000,000 allocated to flood control, in 50 years with interest at 3 percent per annum, and also excluded the All-American Canal from the project. Appropriations in the maximum amount of $165,-000,000 were originally authorized, but construction costs incurred to June 30, 1947 (when 78 percent of the proposed ultimate generating capacity had been installed) amounted to approximately $141,000,000 for Hoover Dam and power plant and $46,000,000 for the All-American Canal. The ultimate cost was estimated as of that date at $165,-000,000 for the dam and power plant and $72,313,501 for the canal. The revenues of the project consist chiefly of charges for energy sold to the lessees, and generating charges assessed against the lessees of the generating equipment. Repayments made to June 30, 1947, on advances for Hoover Dam and power plant were substantially in excess of requirements, on the equal-annual-installment basis with interest compounded at 3 percent per annum, due to advance payments received from lessees of the generating equipment, but the repayment report indicates that net revenues to that date were $4,762,631 short of repayment requirements. If this deficiency is adjusted by adding $1,514,610, representing prepaid revenues for which repayment credit has been taken, and $4,723,041 of additional provision for replacements, based on the requirements of Federal Power Commission Administrative Memorandum No. 12, and by deducting $704,070, representing the net interest effect of the above and other minor adjustments and the interest credit for repayments in excess of revenues, the cumulative deficiency at June 30, 1947, would amount to $10,296,212.

**39**

Further details with respect to this project are given in a separate report in a later section of this report.

## SUMMARY AS TO BUREAU OF RECLAMATION PROJECTS

In our reports on the individual Bureau of Reclamation projects and in the summaries which follow, we usually report only on the amounts of the costs to be repaid by power revenues omitting reference to the estimated amounts which will be repaid by water users.

In spite of the frequently published statements to the effect that all Bureau of Reclamation projects are repaying the investment with interest, it will be seen from the summaries as to individual projects which follow that, of the 14 projects, only 7 can be regarded as meeting the equal-annual-payment test in 50 years with 3 percent interest (as to one of these—Fort Peck—the Federal Power Commission has raised a question as to whether continued low flows of water will not reduce the estimated revenues) ; the other 7 will not meet this repayment test.

It may be of interest that of the seven which meet the test referred to, power was first produced as to six of them from 1909 to 1932 and, as to the seventh, in 1943, and that, as to those that do not meet the test, power was first produced in one in 1912, one in 1922, and in the remaining five from 1939 to 1944.

More important, as will appear in the next few pages, the prospective deficiencies of the projects which do not meet the test greatly outweigh the prospective surpluses of those which do.

Summaries, as to individual projects, of the results of our tests of ability to repay investments in Bureau of Reclamation projects follow:

### Boise Project

This project was first authorized as an irrigation project in 1905 and power first became available in 1912. Total construction costs to June 30, 1947, were $44,104,422. After elimination of projects which relate entirely to irrigation, the remaining costs are $22,833,990. It is estimated that this amount will be increased to $35,616,192 when construction is completed in 1950. Of this total estimated cost, an amount of $16,862,460 has been allocated as repayable from power revenues, $12,832,250 has been allocated to flood control and the balance is to be repaid by water users. In order to repay the investment of $16,862,460 allocated as repayable from power revenues in equal annual payments in 50 years, with interest at 3 percent compounded annually, annual revenues of $655,368 would be required. The estimated net revenues of $254,942 are, therefore, insufficient and would result in an annual deficiency of $400,426.

**40**

## Minidoka Project

This project was authorized in 1904. Total construction costs to June 30, 1947, were $23,052,430, of which amount $2,032,185 is to be repaid from power revenues. Accumulated power revenues, as reported, are more than sufficient to repay that portion of the investment in 50 years, with interest at 3 percent compounded annually.

## Yakima Project

This project was authorized in 1905 and a power plant was added in 1932. Total construction costs to June 30, 1947, were $39,477,061. The repayment studies show that an amount of $600,843 is to be repaid from power revenues, and the remainder is repayable by water users over periods extending up to 100 years. Net revenues from power for the 15 years 1933 to 1947, inclusive, are more than sufficient to repay the costs allocated to power in equal annual payments over 50 years, with interest at 3 percent compounded annually.

## Central Valley Project

This project was authorized in 1935 and construction began in 1937. The ultimate cost is estimated at $411,000,000, of which it is estimated that approximately $53,000,000 will be allocated to navigation and flood control as nonreimbursable, $130,000,000 will be repayable by water users, and $228,000,000 will be repayable from power revenues. The equal annual amount required to amortize in 50 years the investment of $228,000,000 repayable from power revenues, with interest at 3 percent compounded annually, would be $8,861,334. The estimated average annual power revenues of $3,506,123 would thus result in an average annual deficiency of $5,355,211. The repayment studies make no actual provision for interest while purporting to do so and to that extent may mislead the reader. It may also be pointed out that they show a surplus in the year 2005 of almost $3,000,000 whereas, in reality, on the basis of the studies themselves no such surplus will exist.

Further details of this project are given in an individual report later herein.

## Parker-Davis Project

Construction of Davis Dam, which will be the principal investment of the Government in this project, was authorized in 1941 but was delayed on account of the war, and the power plant was not in operation at June 30, 1947. Ultimate total construction cost is estimated at $127,691,777, of which amount $38,296,614 had been expended at June 30, 1947. The repayment studies show that the average revenues

**41**

from the year 1956 through 2005 are expected to be $3,949,065. The eventual investment to be repaid from power revenues is estimated at $115,363,300. An equal annual payment of $4,483,652 is required to repay that investment in 50 years with interest at 3 percent, compounded annually, an annual deficiency of $534,587 thus being indicated.

## Yuma Project

This project was authorized for irrigation only in 1904 and power features were added in 1926. The revenues from power operations have been sufficient to repay the total investment of $554,022 to be repaid from power revenues and to provide a small surplus at June 30, 1947. Total construction costs to June 30, 1947, were $10,275,467.

## Grand Valley Project

This project was authorized in 1912 and a power plant was constructed with funds advanced by the Public Service Co. of Colorado. The company operates the plant and pays an annual rental of $12,000 to the United States, which amount is applied toward repayment of irrigation construction charges. The Bureau of Reclamation estimates that, by 1973, payments by water users and net power revenues will have repaid the total investment applicable to water of $4,156,663, except for an amount of $1,270,808, representing contract obligations against lands considered temporarily unproductive. In addition to this unpaid amount, no interest will have been collected on the Government's investment in this project.

## Rio Grande Project

This project was approved in 1905 and power features were constructed in 1938–40. The repayment studies for the fiscal year 1947 show that the net revenues of $217,673 are $98,588 less than the amount required to repay the investment repayable from power revenues of $8,137,320 (representing 38 percent of total construction cost to June 30, 1947) in 50 years, with interest at 3 percent compounded annually. Furthermore, in the year 1966, when ultimate expenditures to be repaid from power revenues of $11,000,000 are reached, the annual net revenues will be $113,661 less than the required amount on the above basis. No adjustment has been made in these computations with respect to the provision for replacements which provision appears to be insufficient.

## Riverton Project

This project was approved in 1918. Total construction costs to June 30, 1947, are stated at $7,009,834 of which $661,277 is repayable from power revenues. These revenues, it now appears, will be sufficient to repay this $661,277 in 50 years, with interest at 3 percent, compounded annually.

### Shoshone and Heart Mountain Project

This project was authorized in 1904 and the first revenues from power operations were received in the year 1922. The repayment studies of the Bureau of Reclamation show that to June 30, 1947, the accumulated net revenues of $1,433,569 are $1,206,845 less than the amount required to that date to repay the amount repayable from power revenues ($3,092,747 of the total construction costs of $15,639,023) on a 50-year equal-annual-payment basis, with interest at 3 percent, compounded annually, and that, by the year 1971, there will, on the same basis, be an accumulated deficiency of $2,492,622.

### Fort Peck Project

This project was authorized in 1938 and the first power revenues were received in the year 1944. The repayment studies of the Bureau of Reclamation show that, upon completion of construction in 1956, $25,800,000 of the total construction cost (which is estimated at $135,500,000) will be repayable from power revenues, and the average annual revenues of $1,126,676 will be $123,946 more than the amount of $1,002,730 which is necessary to repay the investment in equal annual payments in 50 years, with interest at 3 percent, compounded annually. However, the Federal Power Commission, in its order of April 20, 1943, points out that if the low flows of water experienced in recent years should continue, it might become doubtful whether the estimated power revenues could be realized.

### Colorado-Big Thompson Project

This project was authorized in 1937. It is anticipated that construction of all facilities will be completed by 1955 at an estimated cost of $131,850,665 and that the portion thereof to be repaid from power revenues will be $106,850,665. The annual net revenues, before providing for replacements, as estimated by the Bureau of Reclamation, are $2,540,700. The annual provision for replacements on the basis of Federal Power Commission Administrative Memorandum No. 12 is $679,570, leaving a balance of $1,861,130. The amount required to repay the investment (including an additional amount of $6,411,040 representing estimated interest during construction) to be repaid from power revenues in equal annual payments over a 50-year period, with interest at 3 percent, compounded annually, is $4,401,973. Thus, from 1956 through 1993 (the last year of the 50-year amortization period for the first facilities put in service) the estimated annual deficiency will amount to $2,540,843. In fact, the estimated annual earnings will

**43**

be sufficient to pay only about 55 percent of the interest on the investment without any provision for amortization.

Further details of this project are given in an individual report later herein.

### Kendrick Project

This project was authorized in 1933 and power operations commenced in 1940. The total construction costs to June 30, 1947, were $18,248,970. While the repayment studies indicate sufficient revenues to that date to amortize the investment with interest, they are not indicative of the ultimate results because the total cost to be recovered from power revenues is shown as $7,090,988 while the corresponding figure in 1956 is expected to reach $22,400,000, principally through recognition, for the first time, of an amount of $12,870,973 representing irrigation costs to be repaid from power revenues, and further because the revenues after 1952 will be reduced to $364,400 as compared with $457,082 for 1947. The equal annual payment required to amortize the investment of $22,400,000 in 50 years at 3 percent interest, compounded annually, is $870,587 as compared with estimated net revenues of $364,400, thus indicating an annual deficiency, after the next few years, of $506,187.

### North Platte Project

This project was authorized in 1903 and the repayment studies show that the total investment to be recovered from power revenues ($2,-274,772 of total construction costs of $19,564,134) was repaid in 1941.

### COLUMBIA RIVER POWER SYSTEM, CONSISTING OF BONNEVILLE DAM PROJECT, COLUMBIA BASIN PROJECT (GRAND COULEE DAM), AND BONNEVILLE POWER ADMINISTRATION

Construction of Bonneville Dam (built and operated by the Corps of Engineers) and Grand Coulee Dam (Columbia Basin project) (built and operated by the Bureau of Reclamation), was begun in 1933 with public works funds, and the projects were formally authorized by the Congress in 1935. The first generating units were placed in operation at Bonneville Dam in 1938, and the last unit in 1943. The first generating unit at Grand Coulee Dam was placed in operation in 1941, and at June 30, 1947, 6 of the 18 proposed generating units were in service. The proposed irrigation works of the Columbia Basin project were still in the early stages of construction at June 30, 1947. The Bonneville Power Administration, an agency of the Department of the Interior, was authorized in 1937 for the purpose of transmitting and selling the power generated at Bonneville Dam, and the President, in 1940, designated the Administration to perform the same function for Grand Coulee Dam.

The funds made available for construction and operation of these projects to June 30, 1947, totaled $442,765,756, nearly all of which represents appropriations of general and emergency funds. The Federal Power Commission, in 1945, determined that one-half of the cost of construction of joint facilities at Bonneville Dam, including construction interest at $2\frac{1}{2}$ percent should be allocated to navigation and one-half to power, the latter to be repaid over 50 years with interest at $2\frac{1}{2}$ percent. The Bureau of Reclamation and the Bonneville Power Administration have allocated the construction cost of joint facilities at Grand Coulee Dam (no construction interest included for repayment purposes) as follows: $1,000,000 to navigation and flood control; 44 percent of the balance to irrigation; and the remaining 56 percent of the balance to power. Of the balance allocated to power, one-half was allocated to downstream river regulation benefits determined to be applicable to dams still to be constructed and to Grand Coulee Dam. Since Grand Coulee Dam was authorized under the Reclamation Project Act of 1939, and because anticipated payments by water users are far short of the specific and joint construction costs to be allocated to irrigation, the construction costs allocated to power for repayment purposes include not only the construction costs allocated to power, but also the joint construction costs allocated to irrigation and approximately 65 percent ($233,000,-000) of the proposed specific irrigation construction costs (based on 1945 prices). The repayment schedule for Grand Coulee Dam provides interest at 3 percent only on construction costs allocated to power. The repayment period for construction costs of Grand Coulee Dam allocated to power for repayment extends over 86 years to the year 2028, on the basis of 1945 prices. All construction costs of the Bonneville Power Administration, including construction interest at $2\frac{1}{2}$ percent, are allocated to power, and are to be repaid, with interest at $2\frac{1}{2}$ percent over periods of 50 years from the dates the assets were placed in service.

The 1947 repayment report indicates, on the basis of the repayment requirements set forth above, and by deferring to future periods (1) the repayment of joint construction costs allocated to downstream river regulation benefits to dams still to be constructed and (2) the repayment of construction costs allocated to irrigation but allocated to power for repayment, that repayments to June 30, 1947, were in excess of requirements by $152,282 for Bonneville Dam, $3,702,545 for Grand Coulee Dam, and $10,182,590 for the Bonneville Power Administration, or a total of $14,037,417. It is estimated that if the repayment requirements for Grand Coulee Dam were computed on the same basis as those for Bonneville Dam and Bonneville Power Administration, by including construction interest at $2\frac{1}{2}$ percent and by paying interest at $2\frac{1}{2}$ percent and amortizing construction cost on all facilities allocated to power for repayment from the date such facilities are put in service, the combined excess of repayments over requirements for all three projects, as shown above, would be reduced by more than $7,500,000.

The investment section of the statement of combined assets and liabilities allocated to power, in the annual financial reports, includes appropriations for operation and maintenance in the gross investment of the Government and includes repayments of such expenses under funds returned to the Treasury. Also, that portion of the investment in facilities allocated to irrigation which is allocated to power for repayment is excluded from the statement of combined assets and liabilities allocated to power. As a result of the above, the impression is given that approximately 28 percent of the Government's investment had been repaid at June 30, 1947. If operation and maintenance expenses were excluded from the gross investment and from repayments and if the investment in all facilities allocated to power for repayment were included in the gross investment, the actual repayments to June 30, 1947, would be approximately 9 percent of the investment in facilities allocated to power for repayment.

For further details reference is made to the individual report on this project.

## SOUTHWESTERN POWER ADMINISTRATION

The total investment to June 30, 1947, was $82,927,368. No allocations of costs have been made, though it is indicated that some portion of the total costs may be allocated to flood control, navigation, and river regulation. In the absence of such allocations, our computation is made on the basis that all costs will be repaid from power revenues.

The income available for such purposes in 1947 was $374,407, or less than one-half of 1 percent of the total investment. The total income required for that year to amortize the investment in equal annual payments, in 50 years, with 2½ percent interest compounded annually, is $2,873,471.

The cumulative results to June 30, 1947, are as follows:

Payments required on the above basis_____ $8,431,900
Total credit with Treasury available for repayment_____ 398,804

Deficiency_____ 8,033,096
Add 2½ percent interest on deficiency at the close of
each fiscal year_____ 216,064

Cumulative excess of required annual payments over
available credit with Treasury_____ 8,249,160

An individual report on this project is presented later.

**46**

The Tennessee Valley Authority was created by an act of Congress, approved May 18, 1933. At June 30, 1947, 16 multiple-use dams, 12 single-use (for power) dams, 10 steam plants, and extensive transmission, navigation, and chemical facilities had been constructed, purchased from utilities companies, or acquired from other departments or agencies of the Government, and two major multiple-use dams were under construction. The generating capacity of the system at June 30, 1947, was 2,538,902 kilowatts and 402,600 kilowatts of additional capacity were under construction.

The Authority is a corporation without capital stock and is managed by a Board of three directors, appointed by the President with the advice and consent of the Senate. The Authority is audited annually by the General Accounting Office but, by amendment of the act in 1941, the Congress prohibited the GAO from disallowing credit or withholding funds because of any expenditure which the board of directors shall determine to have been necessary to carry out the provisions of the act. The Authority was made subject to the provisions of the Government Corporation Control Act, which was approved on December 6, 1945, and since that time has been subject to a business-type audit by the GAO.

The Authority is required to make payments in lieu of taxes to the State and local governments in which the power operations are carried on, beginning at 10 percent of gross power sales for the fiscal year beginning July 1, 1940, to customers other than agencies and departments of the Government and gradually decreasing to 5 percent of such sales for the fiscal year beginning July 1, 1948, and thereafter.

As of June 30, 1947, Government funds from new appropriations and bonds sold to the Treasury and the Reconstruction Finance Corporation, and the assigned value of properties transferred from other Government departments or agencies totaled $822,831,346, including an amount of $33,883,322, representing unused appropriations at that date. In addition, funds in the amount of approximately $131,692,-600, consisting of the excess of net power revenues (before provisions for depreciation and for amortization of acquisition cost adjustments) over repayments to the Treasury (exclusive of interest on bonded indebtedness), had been retained by the Authority as working capital or for reinvestment in new facilities.

The allocation of joint construction costs is made by the board of directors. At June 30, 1947, 40 percent of such joint costs were allocated to power and 30 percent each to navigation and flood control.

The GAO has recommended that a new allocation study be made, inasmuch as it does not consider that the present allocation of costs to navigation and flood control is justified.

The gross investment in facilities allocated to power at June 30, 1947, excluding depreciation reserves at dates of acquisition and including all acquisition cost adjustments, amounted to $471,545,226, based on the latest allocation report of multiple-use construction in progress allocable to power. Inasmuch as a large part of the net power revenues before provisions for depreciation and for amortization of acquisition cost adjustments were retained by the Authority, it is necessary to assume that such net revenues retained were, in effect, repaid to the Treasury and reappropriated. The addition of construction interest, which we have estimated at $21,992,707, would increase the cost of facilities allocated to power at June 30, 1947, as shown above, to $493,537,933, of which $468,174,004 represents facilities in service and $25,363,929 represents construction in progress. The net power revenues available for debt repayment to June 30, 1947, have been estimated to be $145,855,400, consisting of reported net revenues adjusted by (1) adding back the noncash provisions for depreciation and for amortization of cost acquisition adjustments, (2) adding back interest paid on the funded debt, (3) deducting the estimated required provision for replacements, and (4) adding the estimated interest credit on net cash revenues and on the excess of the above provision for replacements over the net cost of retirements. The above estimated net power revenues available for debt repayment are $47,060,917 in excess of the revenues which would have been required to amortize the investment allocated to power facilities on the basis of equal annual payments, including interest at 3 percent over periods of 50 years from the dates the facilities were placed in service. On the same basis the excess for the fiscal year 1947 amounted to $10,058,797.

If each year's net power revenues available for debt repayment, computed as above, are reduced by interest at 3 percent on the unpaid balance of the investment in facilities allocated to power, and the remainder applied to reduce such unpaid balance, the unpaid balance of the investment in power facilities at June 30, 1947, exclusive of construction in progress, amounts to $393,261,454. Under the provisions of the Government Corporations Appropriation Act for 1948, the Authority is presently required to repay $348,239,240 during the 40 years beginning July 1, 1947, on the power investment at that date. Repayment of the debt balance of $393,261,454 at June 30, 1947, in 40 equal annual payments, with interest at 3 percent would require total payments of $680,537,058 which amount is $332,297,818 greater than the $348,239,240 presently required to be repaid.

Further details will be found in an accompanying individual report on this project.

# Considerations Other Than Financial Results and Comparison of Government-Owned With Privately Owned Projects

In presenting the foregoing financial analyses of various power projects, it should be understood that we are not suggesting that nothing beyond financial considerations should be taken into account in determining national policy in general, or the desirability of any particular project. There are many other considerations, which are outside of our field as accountants, and on which we are not professionally qualified to express an opinion.

With respect to these other considerations, it is pertinent to note some of the differences between Government-owned and privately owned power enterprises:

*Government-owned Power Projects*

Projects are usually built to serve more than one purpose, such as flood control, navigation, irrigation, generation of power, etc. In general, power production is considered to be incidental to the other purposes.

By law, the administrators of power marketing are required to charge the lowest rates consistent with cost, in order to encourage the widespread use of power.

Projects are exempt from taxation, except where payments in lieu of State and local taxes are required by law.

Under reclamation law, power revenues are sometimes used to supplement payment by water users on account of irrigation costs.

Government procedures tend to hamper efficient management. Appropriation procedures, and the limitations thereof, are not conducive to economical administration of a construction or an operating program.

*Privately Owned Power Projects*

Projects are built to maximize economies of power supply and other purposes are usually subordinate and incidental.

Management is expected to produce maximum earnings while meeting the requirements of public regulation. Levels of earnings are important measures of managerial success.

The Federal Power Commission has reported for the year 1946 that Federal, State, and local taxes for all class A and B utilities in the United States averaged 19 percent of gross revenues or 5 percent of gross plant investments.

There is no such requirement.

Flexible management tools are available and management is judged, in part, by its ability to make efficient use of them.

Projects are financed from public funds and interest charges thereon are not usually made. If interest were charged at the average rate of all Government securities now outstanding, the rate would be about 2.20 percent.

The cost of funds raised through the sale of bonds or preferred stock would generally be considerably higher than 2.20 percent.

There may be substantial benefits other than revenues to the Government, such as those arising from flood control and navigation.

Projects are built primarily for power purposes and other purposes are incidental. However, Federal licensees may be required to contribute to other purposes, such as flood control and navigation.

# II. THE RECLAMATION FUND

## History

The Reclamation Act of June 17, 1902, committed the Government to a national reclamation policy. Instead of financing reclamation work with direct appropriations from the Federal Treasury (the usual method adopted by Congress to finance Government activities), the act created the "reclamation fund," a revolving fund, by reserving, setting aside, and appropriating to this fund moneys received from the sale and disposal of public lands in 16 Western States and Territories (beginning with the fiscal year 1901) to be used in the examination and survey for, and the construction and maintenance of, irrigation works for the storage, diversion, and development of waters for the reclamation of arid and semiarid lands in the said States and Territories. In 1906 Congress extended the reclamation act to include the State of Texas.

The proceeds of sales of lands in these States and Territories were deposited in one fund, which could be used only for reclamation projects in the same States and Territories. However, the fund was not segregated by States and Territories. This feature became more important when, in February 1920, Congress passed the "Oil-Leasing Act," which provided that of the money received from sales, bonuses, royalties, and rentals from the mining of coal, phosphates, oil, oil shale, gas, and sodium on the public domain (excepting in Alaska), 70 percent from past production and 52½ percent from future production should be paid into, reserved, and appropriated as a part of the reclamation fund. Whether or not a particular State contributed any moneys to the fund from these sources, it is nevertheless entitled to participate in the expenditures for reclamation.

Under the Federal Water Power Act of 1920, 50 percent of the charges for Federal water-power licenses for use of public lands is likewise paid into the reclamation fund. In more recent years, it has become the practice to appropriate funds for power and irrigation projects out of general funds and to require that repayments be paid into the reclamation fund.

Though the reclamation fund was set up originally as a revolving fund which could be used without serious restriction for reclamation purposes, the Congress curtailed this latitude by the Reclamation Extension Act of 1914, which provided that no funds could be disbursed from the reclamation fund without an appropriation by the Congress. However, there is evidence that the existence of this fund facilitates action by the Congress in making appropriations therefrom, in spite of the fact that the greater part of the fund has been derived from general funds of the Treasury. Evidence of the attitude of Congress in appropriating funds for the reclamation fund is to be found in the hearings before the Subcommittee of the Committee on Appropriations, House of Representatives, Eightieth Congress, second session on the Interior Department appropriation bill for 1949. In referring to the compliance by Bonneville Power Administration with the requirement of the 1948 appropriations act, that interest be covered into the reclamation fund and not be allocated during the fiscal year 1948, Representative Jensen (Iowa) stated (p. 192):

Thank you. We are glad to have the money. We will be just a little more liberal with all of these folks when money is appropriated for the Interior Department. The more interest we can get in and the more money we can get into the reclamation funds and the Treasury of the United States, the bigger-hearted we are apt to be.

Because it appears possible to overlook the fact that the moneys expended for reclamation projects, most of which comes from general and emergency funds, will, on repayment, go into the reclamation fund, it is recommended that consideration be given to abolishing the fund.

## The Present Status

The assets of the reclamation fund consist of a balance with the Treasury and all reimbursable investments in reclamation projects (including investments in power facilities). The balance with the Treasury of $47,000,000 at June 30, 1947, is probably less than 5 percent of the total estimated assets of the fund. No complete statement of these assets is available or has been published. The available facts indicate that the fund has assets of nearly $1,000,000,000.

Thus the reclamation fund has undergone a substantial metamorphosis since its creation by the Reclamation Act of 1902. Moneys derived from the sale of public lands, from oil leases, and from Federal water-power licenses are minor compared with the contributions from general and emergency funds to reclamation projects which are reimbursable to the reclamation fund. By June 1949, total contributions from general and emergency funds will have reached a total of $1,230,000,000, as shown in a tabulation later in this report.

Up to the year 1930, only $4,500,000 had been so contributed from general funds. Since that date the amounts so contributed have been increasing almost constantly, the largest appropriations from general funds being for the fiscal years 1948 and 1949, in the amounts of $117,000,000 and $211,000,000, respectively.

The Bureau of Reclamation reports total construction expenditures to June 30, 1947, of $1,083,000,000. It also reports that another billion dollars will be required to complete the projects now in process of construction. Presumably, the Congress is expected to appropriate most of this money from general funds.

By appropriating from general funds for Bureau of Reclamation projects the repayments of the reimbursable portion of such funds, with interest paid thereon, if any, become an addition to the reclamation fund. Thus, by far the greatest part of the accretions to the fund will be received, not from the sources originally intended when the reclamation act was passed, but from repayments by projects constructed with general funds, which, when appropriated by the Congress, become a subsidy to the reclamation fund by all of the taxpayers. Furthermore, if all reimbursable investments are repaid over periods of 50 years, with 3 percent interest, on the costs allocated to power for repayment, the amounts repaid to the reclamation fund over those periods will be almost twice the reimbursable amount contributed from the general funds. This is because, in addition to the subsidy of the original contribution, there is a further subsidy of the interest which, over a 50-year repayment period, is almost equal to the principal. These facts should be kept in mind in considering the present program for all proposed power and reclamation projects, which, as stated elsewhere in this report, envisages total expenditures in excess of $40,000,-000,000. If the expenditures for that portion of the program which is proposed by the Bureau of Reclamation are to come out of general funds and be repaid into the reclamation fund, the fund may reach staggering proportions.

Funds were made available to the Bureau of Reclamation to June 30, 1947, from the following sources:

| | | |
|---|---:|---:|
| Reclamation fund | | $461,979,759 |
| General funds of the Treasury | | 709,351,057 |
| Emergency funds | | 192,478,535 |
| Authorizations from power revenues: | | |
| Hoover Dam | $7,665,600 | |
| Other reclamation projects | 16,781,920 | |
| | | 24,447,520 |
| Special fund (sale of land in 1917) | | 15,000 |
| | | 1,388,271,871 |

to which should be added:

| | | |
|---|---:|---:|
| Reclamation fund: | | |
| 1948 | 20,127,250 | |
| 1949 | 27,516,397 | |
| | | 47,643,647 |

General funds:

| | | |
|---|---|---|
| 1948_____ | $117,508,288 | |
| 1949_____ | 211,926,503 | |
| | | $329,434,791 |

Authorizations from power revenues:

| | | |
|---|---|---|
| 1948 reclamation projects_____ | 5,549,500 | |
| 1949 reclamation projects_____ | 6,616,042 | |
| | | 12,165,542 |

Grand total to June 30, 1949_____ 1,777,515,851

Of this total, appropriations for Hoover Dam, for which the repayments to the Treasury will clear through the Colorado River dam fund, amount to $149,394,871.

Authorizations from power revenues, included in the various appropriation bills since 1929, but not included in the totals of amounts appropriated, are in effect additional appropriations from the reclamation fund and are so handled in the accounts of the Bureau of Reclamation. It would appear that there is no valid reason for continuing this method. It gives the impression that the appropriations from the fund are limited to the totals stated in the bills, as actually the additional amounts from power revenues are also appropriated. It is a significant fact that this practice was stopped in 1947 with respect to the Colorado River dam fund, through which appropriations for Hoover Dam are processed.

Collections from water users for construction charges and of net revenues from power operations, exclusive of Hoover Dam, are stated to be approximately $120,000,000 to June 30, 1947. While these collections are regarded as the extent to which the reclamation fund has recovered its investment, it should be pointed out that the amount of $120,000,000 is far short of equaling simple interest at 3 percent per annum on the amounts contributed to the reclamation fund from general and emergency funds.

Appropriations from general funds and emergency funds, from the inception of the reclamation fund, are tabulated below:

| Year: | General Fund | Emergency Funds | Year: | General Fund | Emergency Funds |
|---|---|---|---|---|---|
| 1907__ | $1,000,000 | _____ | 1931__ | 10,760,000 | _____ |
| 1918__ | 310,213 | _____ | 1932__ | 15,100,000 | _____ |
| 1919__ | 443,196 | _____ | 1933__ | 23,050,000 | _____ |
| 1920__ | 548,927 | _____ | 1934__ | 8,048,000 | $87,205,098 |
| 1921__ | 661,177 | _____ | 1935__ | _____ | 30,523,787 |
| 1922__ | 335,871 | _____ | 1936__ | 14,050,000 | 36,883,746 |
| 1923__ | 559,530 | _____ | 1937__ | 43,750,000 | 1,646,362 |
| 1924__ | 314,067 | _____ | 1938__ | 30,570,000 | 31,089,515 |
| 1926__ | 50,000 | _____ | 1939__ | 32,995,000 | 2,376,654 |
| 1927__ | 75,000 | _____ | 1940__ | 63,715,000 | 2,715,032 |
| 1928__ | 50,000 | _____ | 1941__ | 63,765,000 | 13,517 |
| 1929__ | 115,000 | _____ | 1942__ | 93,915,031 | 24,824 |
| 1930__ | 100,000 | _____ | 1943__ | 87,076,210 | _____ |

| Year: | General Fund | Emergency Funds | Year: | General Fund | Emergency Funds |
|---|---|---|---|---|---|
| 1944__ | $35, 853, 000 | _____ | 1948__ | $117, 508, 288 | _____ |
| 1945__ | 19, 324, 200 | _____ | 1949__ | 211, 926, 503 | _____ |
| 1946__ | 84, 470, 500 | _____ | | | |
| 1947__ | 78, 346, 135 | _____ | Total_ | 1, 038, 785, 848 | $192, 478, 535 |
| | 709, 351, 057 | $192, 478, 535 | | | |

Combined_____ $1, 231, 264, 383

We recognize that the foregoing report on the present status of the reclamation fund is incomplete. However, it represents all of the pertinent information we have been able to secure. In particular, it is lacking in a reconcilement of the total funds of $1,777,515,851 made available to the Bureau of Reclamation with the expenditures incurred. A complete report would include a statement of all expenditures, showing separately construction expenditures and administrative expenses and would further break down the construction expenditures into those which are reimbursable and nonreimbursable.

In the recommendations included in the introductory statement to this report, we recommend that a complete report along the lines above indicated be prepared and submitted to the Congress.

# III. REPORTS ON INDIVIDUAL GOVERNMENT-OWNED HYDROELECTRIC PROJECTS

## Boulder Canyon Project (Hoover Dam)

*(Department of the Interior—Bureau of Reclamation)*

AUTHORIZATION

The Boulder Canyon Project Act, approved December 21, 1928, authorized construction of the Boulder Canyon project, consisting of a dam, a power plant, and a canal, and established the Colorado River dam fund to finance the construction thereof. The purposes of the project were stated to be control of floods, improving navigation and regulating the flow of the Colorado River, storage and delivery of water for reclamation of public lands, and for generation of electrical energy as a means of making the project self-supporting and financially solvent.

Construction of the dam and power plant was begun on March 11, 1931, and the structure was completed 5 years later, being accepted by the Secretary of the Interior on March 1, 1936. Generation of power was formally initiated on September 11, 1936.

APPROPRIATIONS

The Boulder Canyon Project Act provided that all revenues and advances of appropriations for construction were to be paid into and all expenditures made out of the Colorado River dam fund under the direction of the Secretary of the Interior. The effect of this provision would have been to give the agency greater flexibility in handling funds than is allowed the ordinary Government agency which normally is required to cover all receipts into the Treasury as miscellaneous receipts and to obtain funds for operation and maintenance through appropriations. However, from the beginning of operations, the Congress set a limit each year on the amount of the fund which could be used for operation and maintenance and the Bouler Canyon Project Adjustment Act, approved July 19, 1940, provided that annual appropriations be made from the fund for operation, maintenance, and replacements of the project.

The Boulder Canyon Project Act authorized the appropriation for construction of the project of general funds of the Treasury not to exceed an aggregate amount of $165,000,000. However, total funds made available for construction to June 30, 1947, aggregated $186,-580,103, consisting of $140,754,941 for Hoover Dam and power plant and $45,825,162 for the All-American Canal, from the following sources:

| | Hoover Dam and power plant | All-American Canal |
|---|---|---|
| General funds of the Treasury_____ | $109, 418, 355 | $26, 000, 000 |
| Emergency funds_____ | 30, 996, 586 | 19, 825, 162 |
| Total construction funds from Government appropriations_____ | 140, 414, 941 | 45, 825, 162 |
| Advances by outsiders for construction_____ | 340, 000 | ----------- |
| Total construction funds made available to June 30, 1947_____ | 140, 754, 941 | 45, 825, 162 |

At May 31, 1947, the capacity of the generating units was 1,036,000 kilovolt-amperes, which was 78 percent of the proposed ultimate installation of 1,323,500 kilovolt-amperes. The ultimate cost of the project, as set forth in the hearings for the 1949 appropriation bill, is now estimated to be $165,000,000 for the dam and power plant and $72,313,501 for the All-American Canal.

REPAYMENT REQUIREMENTS

The Boulder Canyon Project Act provided that before any money was appropriated for construction of the dam or power plant, the Secretary of the Interior was required to make provision for revenues by contract adequate to insure payment of all expenses of operation and maintenance and the repayment within 50 years from the date of completion of all amounts advanced to the fund, except $25,000,000 allocated to flood control, together with interest at 4 percent per annum. Contracts for the sale of electrical energy were to be made with a view to obtaining reasonable returns and provision was made for adjustment of rates when justified by competitive conditions. If any revenues were received in excess of repayment requirements, 62½ percent of such excess was to be applied in reduction of the advances allocated to flood control and 37½ percent was to be paid in equal amounts to the States of Arizona and Nevada. Provision was also made for the Secretary of the Interior to lease units of the power plant with the right to generate electrical energy or to lease the use of the water for the generation of electrical energy.

The Boulder Canyon Project Adjustment Act, approved July 19, 1940, and fully effective May 29, 1941, excluded the All-American Canal from the project and amended the repayment provisions and the basis for energy rate determination by requiring the Secretary of

**57**

the Interior to promulgate energy charges to provide revenues sufficient, with other net revenues of the project, to meet the cost of operation, maintenance, and replacements, to repay construction costs of the project, exclusive of the $25,000,000 allocated to flood control, with interest at 3 percent per annum, on a 50-year basis, and to provide $300,000 annually to be paid to each of the States of Arizona and Nevada and $500,000 annually to be paid into the Colorado River development fund. Advances made prior to June 1, 1937, are to be repaid by May 31, 1987, and subsequent advances are to be repaid over such 50-year periods as the Secretary may determine. The Senate committee's report on the bill which became the Boulder Canyon Project Adjustment Act stated that the power rates set in 1930 under the original act were excessive due to a decrease in the competitive value of power because of improvements in the art of generating power by steam and decreases in fuel and construction costs. This report also pointed out that the area served by the project was paying excessive rates because in the case of other projects, such as Tennessee Valley Authority and Bonneville, the competitive rate basis had been abandoned in favor of a rate based on recovery of costs allocable to power, and that this policy was made general in the Reclamation Project Act of 1939. The new rates established under the Boulder Canyon Project Adjustment Act by the "General Regulations for Generation and Sale of Power" hereinafter referred to were approximately 29 percent lower than those established in 1930 and were made retroactive to June 1, 1937.

The Boulder Canyon Project Adjustment Act also provided for the termination of the existing lease of generating facilities and their subsequent operation by the lessees as agents of the United States. Pursuant to these provisions, contracts subsequently were made with the city of Los Angeles and Southern California Edison Co., Ltd., to operate the generating machinery and equipment as agents.

The Boulder Canyon Project Adjustment Act also provided that repayment of the $25,000,000 allocated to flood control be deferred without interest until June 1, 1987, and be repaid after that date to the Treasury as the Congress may direct.

On May 20, 1941, the Secretary of the Interior issued the "General Regulations for Generation and Sale of Power in Accordance with the Boulder Canyon Project Adjustment Act." These regulations provide that the charges for electrical energy shall consist of two components, the energy charge and the generating charge, and shall apply retroactively to June 1, 1937. The energy rates, together with the revenues from the sale of stored water, are to be sufficient, but not more than sufficient, to provide:

1. The operation and maintenance costs of those parts of the project not operated by the agents;

58

2. Provision for replacements costing $5,000 or more on the dam and appurtenant works, estimated to be equivalent to an annuity of 1¼ percent of the cost of those features requiring replacement, exclusive of penstocks, and $6,640 for penstocks, subject to revision annually;

3. $300,000 annually to each of the States of Arizona and Nevada;

4. $500,000 annually to the Colorado River development fund; and

5. The annuity required to repay to the Treasury, with interest, advances made to the fund prior to June 1, 1937 (less revenues during the construction period, the $25,000,000 allocated to flood control, and the costs of generating machinery and equipment) within 50 years from that date, and advances made subsequent to that date (excluding the costs of generating machinery and equipment) over periods of 50 years from the subsequent June 1.

### The generating charges are to consist of:

1. The annuity required to repay to the Treasury, with interest, the costs of generating machinery and equipment paid out of advances prior to June 1, 1937, in 50 years from that date and the costs of generating machinery and equipment paid out of advances subsequent to that date over periods of 50 years from the first of the month following the date placed in service.

2. Provision for replacements costing $3,000 or more for any item or part of a 40,000 kilovolt-ampere generating unit and equipment or $5,000 or more for any other replacement, estimated to be an annuity of 1¼ percent of the cost of generating machinery and equipment.

3. The operation and maintenance costs of that portion of the power plant operated and maintained by operating agents.

The schedules for determination of energy rates and generating charges indicate that the annuities required to repay advances or costs, with 3 percent interest, were determined to consist of equal annual installments, which are computed at 3.88655 percent of the total advances or costs (or higher rates for additions to generating facilities in service which must be repaid in less than 50 years), the rate of 3.88655 percent being that required for a 3 percent, 50-year basis. The official reports on the Boulder Canyon project show that it has repaid to the Treasury more than would be required under the equal-annual-payment method over 50 years at 3 percent interest. It is apparent, however, that this was accomplished principally through the collection of an advance payment from the city of Los Angeles of $8,000,000 in the fiscal year 1945. It was therefore necessary for us to make a recomputation comparing net income of the project (after certain adjustments) with the required amortization payments.

Before making this comparison it was necessary to apply the following adjustments to net income as reported:

1. Provisions for replacements are less than required by Federal Power Commission Administrative Memorandum No. 12, dated January 31, 1947. A recomputation was made to show the additional annual amounts required on the basis of that memorandum.

2. Payments to States and the Colorado River development fund and two minor surplus adjustments were applied to the proper year rather than to the year in which recorded.

3. Interest on long-term debt (net of interest on construction) was added back to net income as reported.

4. Interest credit at 3 percent for one-half year on each year's net revenue before provision for replacements was added to net income as reported. Inasmuch as the Treasury has credited the project with interest on repayments from the date of payment to the end of the fiscal year to arrive at the total repayment for each year, a similar credit has been computed on the net revenues before provision for replacements in order to obtain a proper comparison of net revenues with actual repayments and with required amortization payments.

5. Interest credit at 3 percent on the cumulative excess at the beginning of each year of repayments to the Treasury over net revenues before provision for replacements, with interest compounded, was added to net income as reported. (This excess arose from retroactive rate reductions in 1942, from deferment of payments to the States of Arizona and Nevada and the Colorado River development fund, and from advance collections on generating charges from allottees.) While the amount of interest credit so computed is substantially in excess of interest payments made on the advance collections, the full credit has been allowed in order to give the project the benefit of any doubt and because the debt to the Treasury was actually reduced by the full amounts of the repayments made.

No adjustment has been made to include a charge against revenues for Federal, State, and local taxes which would be payable if the project were owned by private interests instead of by the Federal Government. However, it should be noted that the project pays an aggregate of $1,100,000 annually to the States of Arizona and Nevada and the Colorado River development fund, which may be considered as payments in lieu of such taxes.

After giving effect to the foregoing adjustments, the net revenues to May 31, 1947, are compared with the net revenues required under the equal-annual-payment method as follows:

| Period | Adjusted net revenues [1] | Required net revenues | Surplus (deficiency) |
|---|---|---|---|
| Prior to June 1, 1937 | $251, 439 | ‒‒‒‒‒‒‒‒‒‒‒‒‒ | $251, 439 |
| Fiscal year ended May 31: | | | |
| 1938 | (221, 672) | $3, 362, 424 | (3, 584, 096) |
| 1939 | 1, 109, 779 | 3, 593, 753 | (2, 483, 974) |
| 1940 | 1, 840, 262 | 3, 700, 656 | (1, 860, 394) |
| 1941 | 3, 270, 847 | 3, 987, 944 | (717, 097) |
| 1942 | 3, 592, 035 | 4, 114, 211 | (522, 176) |
| 1943 | 4, 166, 831 | 4, 343, 822 | (176, 991) |
| 1944 | 4, 628, 481 | 4, 553, 346 | 75, 135 |
| 1945 | 5, 045, 501 | 4, 629, 158 | 416, 343 |
| 1946 | 4, 723, 140 | 4, 701, 175 | 21, 965 |
| 1947 | 4, 170, 537 | 4, 702, 747 | (532, 210) |
| Total to May 31, 1947 | 32, 577, 180 | 41, 689, 236 | (9, 112, 056) |

[1] After payments to States and Colorado River development fund.

The cumulative deficiency at May 31, 1947, with interest thereon compounded annually at 3 percent per annum, and after allowing a credit each year for interest on the required reserve for replacements, amounted to $10,296,212.

The schedule for determination of energy rates, effective June 1, 1947, prepared by the Bureau of Reclamation, shows a cumulative deficiency at May 31, 1947, of $4,762,631. The difference between this amount and the cumulative deficiency of $10,296,212 shown above is $5,533,581, accounted for as follows:

Additional provision for replacements on basis of Federal Power Commission Administrative Memorandum No. 12 (adjustment No. 1 above) _____ $4,723,041

Prepaid revenues at May 31, 1947, which were applied to reduce the deficit at that date in the schedule for determination of energy rates _____ 1,514,610

Interest on increases in cumulative balance of deficit (net of interest credit on increases in the required reserve for replacements) ____ 700,795

Total _____ 6,938,446

Less:

    Excess of interest allowed on repayments in excess of revenues over interest paid on generating charges collected in advance from allottees (adjustment No. 5 above) _____ $767,334

    Interest credit allowed on each year's net revenues before provision for replacements (adjustment No. 4 above) _____ 587,534

    Miscellaneous _____ 49,997

                               1,404,865

Remainder—Excess of cumulative deficiency as computed over that reported in the schedule for determination of energy rates_____ 5,533,581

The schedules for the determination of energy rates appear to us to have been prepared on basis which conform to the requirements of the law and regulations; it was observed, however, that such schedules do not indicate the time at which full repayment of advances is expected and might, because of their form, lead a reader to the erroneous conclusion that complete repayment may be expected in 1987.

# Central Valley

## (*Department of the Interior—Bureau of Reclamation*)

### AUTHORIZATION

This project was authorized by the Emergency Relief Appropriation Act of 1935 and reauthorized by the Rivers and Harbors Acts of 1937 and 1940. The finding of feasibility was approved by the President December 2, 1935, and construction began in October 1937.

### PURPOSES

The purposes of the project include improvement of navigation, flood control, supplemental water for irrigation through redistribution of the water of the Central Valley between the Sacramento and San Joaquin areas, repulsion of salt water intruding on the delta lands of the Upper San Francisco Bay region, power production, and fresh water for municipal and industrial purposes.

### EXPENDITURES AND REPAYMENT STUDIES

The repayment studies show that in the year 1955 (which appears to be the date of expected completion of construction) the aggregate investment in electric plant and irrigation plant to be repaid from power revenues will be $212,966,476.

Based upon a study of the figures (presented in the repayment studies but which, as to construction costs, are shown later herein to be understated), for that year, 1955, it is apparent that the project will not pay out at the indicated power rates even though approximately $50,000,000 of the construction costs will have been allocated to navigation and flood control as nonreimbursable. The following summary indicates an annual deficiency of $4,702,040:

| | |
|---|---:|
| Electric plant | $104, 143, 600 |
| Irrigation plant | 108, 822, 876 |
| Total to be repaid from power revenues | 212, 966, 476 |
| Amount required to repay in 50 equal annual payments with interest at 3 percent | 8, 277, 048 |
| Net revenue estimated by the Bureau of Reclamation | 3, 575, 008 |
| Annual deficiency | 4, 702, 040 |

In the foregoing computation we have accepted the Bureau of Reclamation's figures for costs, revenues, expenses, and provision for replacements, and we believe that any adjustment which we might suggest would not materially change the result just indicated. Moreover, the Bureau's figures do not provide for interest during construction, and, in view of the result shown, we have not made adjustment therefor.

Total ultimate construction cost, per the repayment studies, is calculated at $384,314,000 as follows:

To be repaid:
| | |
|---|---|
| From power revenues | $212,966,476 |
| By water-users | 121,820,524 |
| Total reimbursable | 334,787,000 |
| Nonreimbursable: Navigation and flood control | 49,527,000 |
| Total | 384,314,000 |

It should be noted that in the hearings on the appropriation bill for 1949 and also in a footnote to the repayment studies, the ultimate estimated cost is increased by $26,771,000, due to higher labor and material costs, to $411,085,000.

If the figures just shown are adjusted proportionately for this increase the adjusted figures would be as follows:

To be repaid:
| | |
|---|---|
| From power revenues | $227,801,547 |
| By water-users | 130,306,442 |
| Total reimbursable | 358,107,989 |
| Nonreimbursable: Navigation and flood control | 52,977,011 |
| Total | 411,085,000 |

Assuming an amount for costs to be repaid from power revenues of $228,000,000, the annual amount required to amortize the investment in 50 years in equal annual instalments with interest at 3 percent compounded annually, would be $8,861,334 against average annual revenues estimated at $3,506,123, resulting in an average annual deficit of $5,355,211.

Our study thus reveals that present and estimated future earnings are not sufficient to repay the investment with interest. Furthermore, the repayment studies, which show that the investment in electric plant and irrigation plant will be repaid by the year 2005, do not provide for the payment of any interest whatsoever, notwithstanding the fact that a column is shown for interest and that computations at 3 percent appear therein aggregating $66,649,016. That amount, in the repayment studies, is used to reduce the investment in irrigation facilities to be repaid from power revenues.

The repayment studies are also open to criticism in that a surplus in the year 2005 of almost $3,000,000 is indicated whereas in reality, on the basis of the studies themselves, no such surplus will exist.

In the above computations, no amount is included as a charge against revenues for Federal, State, and local taxes which would be payable if the project were owned by private interests instead of by the Federal Government.

# Colorado-Big Thompson

*(Department of the Interior—Bureau of Reclamation)*

### APPROPRIATIONS

The Colorado-Big Thompson project was authorized in the Interior Department's Appropriation Act of 1938, approved August 9, 1937, and by the finding of feasibility approved by the President on December 21, 1937. The prime objectives of the project are stated to be the provision of a supplemental irrigation supply for 615,000 acres of land in northeastern Colorado and the development of electric energy for sale to consumers and distributing agencies in Colorado, Wyoming, and Nebraska.

### APPROPRIATIONS

Funds aggregating $38,465,945 had been made available to June 30, 1947, from the following sources:

| | |
|---|---:|
| Reclamation fund: | |
|     Construction | $7, 300, 000 |
|     Operation and maintenance | 830, 800 |
| General funds of the Treasury | 28, 485, 145 |
| Emergency funds | 1, 550, 000 |
| | |
|     Total funds from Government appropriations | 38, 165, 945 |
| Contributions by outsiders in aid of construction | 300, 000 |
| | |
|     Total funds made available | 38, 465, 945 |

### EXPENDITURES

Of the total funds made available, expenditures for construction to June 30, 1947, amounted to $36,276,698, as follows:

| | | |
|---|---:|---:|
| Total funds made available, as above | | $38, 465, 945 |
| Less: | | |
|     Funds appropriated for operation and maintenance | $830, 800 | |
|     Unexpended construction appropriations, available in subsequent year | 2, 550, 782 | |
| | | 3, 381, 582 |
| Remainder | | 35, 084, 363 |
| | | |
| Add items included in construction costs not chargeable to project appropriations | | 1, 192, 335 |
| | | |
|     Total | | 36, 276, 698 |

**65**

Construction began in 1938, and initial production of power occurred in 1943. Water is scheduled to be available for irrigation in 1951. The cost of the project, including irrigation, joint, and power facilities, was originally estimated to be approximately $43,740,000. The revised estimated final cost of the project as stated in hearings in April 1948 is $131,850,665.

The 1938 appropriation act required the Government to enter into repayment contracts with water users before construction was commenced. Accordingly, on July 5, 1938, a contract was entered into between the United States and the Northern Colorado Water Conservancy District providing for the repayment of $22,000,000 with a maximum liability of the district to be $25,000,000 of the construction cost, in 40 annual installments without interest after completion of construction. The only source of repayment of the remainder of the construction cost is power revenues.

Unless the water users agree to an increase in their payments, approximately $107,000,000 of this estimated cost must be recovered from power revenues as compared with an original estimate of approximately $19,000,000, an increase of 463 percent.

Allocations of construction costs to June 30, 1947, and the estimated total cost of completion, excluding interest, and the proposed sources of repayment are as follows:

|  | Cost to June 30, 1947 | Estimated total cost of completion |
|---|---|---|
| Irrigation facilities | $2,872,434 | $35,357,101 |
| Joint facilities | 25,374,661 | 42,191,304 |
| Power facilities | 5,897,332 | 54,302,260 |
| Adjustments | 2,132,271 | ------------ |
| Total | 36,276,698 | 131,850,665 |
| Less amount to be repaid by water users | 2,872,434 | 25,000,000 |
| Remainder—to be repaid from power revenues | 33,404,264 | 106,850,665 |

From the above schedule it is apparent that anticipated payments by water users will approximate 71 percent of the cost of irrigation facilities and that power revenues will be expected to repay the remaining 29 percent.

At June 30, 1947, electric facilities costing $13,488,094 had been placed in service. Since only a fraction of the power and joint facilities and none of the irrigation facilities were in service by June 30, 1947, the Bureau of Reclamation pay-out schedule is the only source of information available for use in estimating whether the project will eventually pay out or not. The pay-out schedule provides less for replacements than is recommended by the Federal Power Commission Administrative Memorandum No. 12, and in addition does not provide for interest during construction on any facilities, or on the completed irrigation costs and unallocated costs to be repaid by power. Moreover, although approximately $42,000,000 of net operating revenues is shown in the pay-out schedules under the caption "Repayment of Investment—Interest 3 percent" this amount is not paid to the United States Treasury as interest, but instead is used to reduce the investment in irrigation plant to be repaid from power revenues. Thus, in effect, the pay-out schedules, while showing columns for interest, and interest-bearing investment, provide for no actual payment of interest on the investment in any of the facilities. On this basis it is indicated that complete repayment of the cost of the project by the year 2001 will be accomplished.

It is anticipated that construction of all facilities will be completed by 1955 and the following summary is based on the final cost as estimated by the Bureau of Reclamation:

Total investment to be repaid from power revenues:

| | |
|---|---:|
| Electric plant | $48, 753, 599 |
| Irrigation plant | 54, 356, 521 |
| Unallocated increases in material and labor costs | 3, 740, 545 |
| Total | 106, 850, 665 |
| Interest during construction based on an average period of construction of 4 years | 6, 411, 040 |
| Total | 113, 261, 705 |

The pay-out schedule prepared by the Bureau of Reclamation indicates that all additions to electric plant and irrigation facilities will be completed in 1955. If provision for replacements is made on the basis of Federal Power Commission Administrative Memorandum No. 12, and if power revenues are required to repay all construction costs not recovered from water users, with interest at 3 percent per annum, the estimated annual deficit from 1956 through 1993 (the last year of the 50-year amortization period for the first facilities put in service) would amount to $2,540,843, computed as follows:

Annual net revenues before providing for replacements, as estimated by the Bureau of Reclamation_____ $2,540,700
Less annual provision for replacements on basis of FPC Administrative Memorandum No. 12 (0.6 percent of $113,261,705)_____ 679,570

Remainder—estimated annual net revenues available for repayment of cost of facilities to be repaid from power revenues_____ 1,861,130
Annual earnings required to repay cost of facilities to be repaid from power revenues in 50 equal annual installments from date of completion, with interest at 3 percent (3.88655 percent of $113,261,705)_____ 4,401,973

Estimated annual deficit (excess of required annual revenues over estimated annual revenues)_____ 2,540,843

Since the annual estimated earnings are not sufficient to pay even the interest on the investment (without any provision for amortization of costs of construction), it is apparent that the project will not pay out at the projected rates and volume of power production.

In the above computations, no amount is included as a charge against revenues for Federal, State, and local taxes which would be payable if the project were owned by private interests instead of by the Federal Government.

According to our computations, revenues as reported for the 4 years ended June 30, 1947, after providing for replacements, resulted in a small surplus over amortization and interest requirements, on the basis of the power facilities in service during that period. However, in these computations, no charge was included for amortization and interest on irrigation construction costs to be repaid from power revenues, with respect to which the Bureau of Reclamation pay-out schedule shows no investment prior to 1951 when an amount of $54,356,521 appears. The pay-out schedule also indicates that after 1956 the costs of irrigation operation and maintenance allocable to power will exceed irrigation pumping revenues by $87,300 annually. Under these conditions the short period of partial operation to June 30, 1947, cannot be regarded as indicative of the eventual performance of the project as a whole.

# Columbia River Power System

*(Department of the Interior)*

*Bonneville Dam Project (Corps of Engineers); Columbia Basin Project (Bureau of Reclamation); Bonneville Power Administration (Department of the Interior)*

AUTHORIZATION

The power projects of the Columbia River Power System which were in operation at June 30, 1947, consist of the Bonneville Dam project (built and operated by the Corps of Engineers, Department of the Army), the Columbia Basin project (Grand Coulee Dam) (built and operated by the Bureau of Reclamation, Department of the Interior), and the Bonneville Power Administration, an agency of the Department of the Interior, which has constructed and operates the transmission system for the sale of power generated by the two dams. A discussion of other projects within the Columbia River Basin, which have been proposed or authorized, or which are under construction but not yet in operation, will be found elsewhere in this report (appendix to parts I, II, and III).

Construction of Bonneville Dam was begun on September 30, 1933, by the Corps of Engineers as a Public Works project. The project was formally authorized by the Congress in the Rivers and Harbors Act of 1935, approved August 30, 1935. The Bonneville Project Act, approved August 20, 1937, stated that the purposes of Bonneville Dam were the improvement of navigation on the Columbia River and other purposes incidental thereto. The first of two generating units, with name-plate ratings of 43,200 kilowatts each, was placed in operation in January 1938 and the last of the additional eight generating units, with name-plate ratings of 54,000 kilowatts each, was placed in service in December 1943. The first recorded sale of power was made in the fiscal year ended June 30, 1939.

Construction of Grand Coulee Dam was begun on December 19, 1933, by the Bureau of Reclamation with money allotted by the Administrator of Public Works pursuant to the authority of title II of the act of June 16, 1933, and additional public works funds were allotted pursuant to the act of April 8, 1935. The Rivers and Harbors Act of 1935 specifically authorized construction, operation, and maintenance of the Grand Coulee Dam project by the President through such agents as he might designate. The President, on January 29, 1936, designated the Secretary of the Interior, acting through the Bureau of Reclamation to act as his agent. The Rivers and Harbors Act of 1935 stated the purposes of this dam, together with Parker Dam, to be control of floods, improvement of navigation, regulation of the flow of streams, storage of water and delivery thereof for the reclamation of public lands and Indian reservations, and other beneficial uses, and for the generation of electric energy as a means of financially aiding and assisting such undertakings. The Columbia Basin Project Act, approved March 10, 1943, recognized the purposes for which the project was authorized by the 1935 act, renamed the project "The Columbia Basin project" and reauthorized it as a project subject to the Reclamation Project Act of 1939. The first of 18 proposed generating units, with name-plate ratings of 108,000 kilowatts each, was placed in operation in September 1941. As of June 30, 1947, six of these units had been in operation since February 1944. In addition, two 75,000-kilowatt generators built for Shasta Dam were temporarily installed in 1943 and removed in 1946. Irrigation works planned in connection with Grand Coulee Dam were still in the early stages of construction at June 30, 1947, approximately 8 percent of the estimated total cost having been incurred at that date.

The Bonneville Power Administration was authorized, as an agency of the Department of the Interior, by the Bonneville Project Act, approved August 20, 1937, for the purposes of constructing and operating transmission lines and other facilities necessary for the transmission of electric energy from Bonneville Dam to existing and potential markets, and of selling such electric energy. On August 26, 1940, the President issued Executive Order No. 8526, designating the Bonneville Power Administrator the agent for the sale and distribution of electrical power and energy generated at the Grand Coulee dam project and not required for operation of that project, including its irrigation features. The order also authorized the Bonneville Power Administrator to construct and operate transmission facilities necessary for marketing the power received from Grand Coulee. Based on the 1947 repayment report, approximately 59 percent of the estimated eventual cost of transmission facilities to be constructed had been incurred at June 30, 1947.

APPROPRIATIONS

All funds for the construction, operation, and maintenance of the Bonneville Dam and Columbia Basin (Grand Coulee Dam) projects and the Bonneville Power Administration have been appropriated or allocated from funds appropriated from general funds of the Treasury by the Congress, except for (1) a $500,000 continuing emergency fund set aside from revenues, and (2) funds for the operation and maintenance costs of the Columbia Basin project which are allocated from funds appropriated to the Bureau of Reclamation from the reclamation fund (some early appropriations for operation and maintenance of this project were also made from general funds of the Treasury). The source of the total funds made available to the three projects through June 30, 1947, is shown in the table on the following page.

SOURCE OF TOTAL FUNDS MADE AVAILABLE TO THE THREE PROJECTS THROUGH JUNE 30, 1947

| | Bonneville Dam project | Columbia Basin project | Bonneville Power Administration | Total |
|---|---|---|---|---|
| General funds of the Treasury: | | | | |
| Specific appropriations | $26,236,000 | $168,597,675 | $115,643,636 | $310,477,311 |
| Allocated from— | | | | |
| Rivers and harbors appropriations | 27,976,976 | --- | --- | 27,976,976 |
| NIRA funds | 20,240,700 | 47,055,000 | --- | 67,295,700 |
| PWA funds | 12,200,000 | --- | 10,750,000 | 22,950,000 |
| WPA funds | --- | 2,920,977 | 5,038,382 | 7,959,359 |
| Reclamation Fund—allocated from funds appropriated to the Bureau of Reclamation | --- | 3,876,256 | --- | 3,876,256 |
| Net transfers from (to) other projects | 175,400 | 1,830,802 | (89,488) | 1,916,714 |
| Total funds from Government appropriations | 86,829,076 | 224,280,710 | 131,342,530 | 442,452,316 |
| Contributions in aid of construction—State of Washington | --- | 313,440 | --- | 313,440 |
| Total funds made available | 86,829,076 | 224,594,150 | 131,342,530 | 442,765,756 |

Pursuant to authority set forth in the Bonneville Project Act, the Federal Power Commission issued an order dated June 26, 1945, allocating to power, as capital investment to be amortized out of revenues from Bonneville power, the capital costs incurred to June 30, 1944, for transmission facilities for the marketing of power from the dam and for specific power facilities at the dam, and one-half of the capital costs incurred to June 30, 1944, for facilities having joint value for the production of electric energy and other purposes. Inasmuch as no supplemental allocations of costs incurred since June 30, 1944, had been made at June 30, 1947, the allocation basis remained the same at that date. Commissioner Nelson Lee Smith dissented from this order on the basis that the project actually is primarily a power project and that navigation cannot reasonably bear 50 percent of the joint costs, and concluded that power might fairly bear 85 percent of the joint costs. In addition, the Federal Power Commission determined that construction costs incurred should include interest during construction at the rate of $2\frac{1}{2}$ percent per annum, being the approximate weighted average cost of money to the United States obtained by the issuance of bonds during the period from 1933 to 1943, inclusive.

The Columbia Basin Project Act reauthorized Grand Coulee Dam as a project subject to the Reclamation Project Act of 1939, and, therefore, allocation of costs and the determination of rates for the sale of electric energy are subject to the provisions of that act. Pursuant thereto, the Secretary of the Interior approved on January 31, 1945, and transmitted to the House of Representatives on May 8, 1945, a Joint Report on Allocation and Repayment of the Costs of the Columbia Basin Project (by the Bureau of Reclamation and Bonneville Power Administration) (79th Cong., 1st sess., H. Doc. No. 172). This report determined, on the basis of the "alternative-justifiable-expenditure" approach (explained in such report), that $1,000,000 of the construction cost of facilities having joint value for the production of electric energy, irrigation, navigation, flood control, and other purposes was allocable to flood control and navigation, and therefore nonreimbursable; that 44 percent of the remaining joint costs was allocable to irrigation; that the remaining 56 percent of joint costs (exclusive of the aforesaid nonreimbursable costs of $1,000,000) was allocable to power; that 50 percent of the joint costs allocable to power represent downstream river regulation benefits to other projects; and that 13.75 percent of the joint costs allocable to downstream river regulation benefits are allocable to the Bonneville Dam Project. The allocation at June 30, 1947, of construction costs incurred to that date is approximately in the ratios indicated above.

## Determination of Electric Energy Rates

Schedules of rates and charges for the sale of electric energy produced at Bonneville Dam have been prepared and issued by the Bonneville Power Administrator and approved by the Federal Power Commission, in accordance with the requirements of the Bonneville Project Act. In the Report on the Columbia Basin Project on the Columbia River (79th Cong., 1st sess. H. Doc. No. 172, referred to previously) the Secretary of the Interior determined that the rates of the Bonneville Power Administration (for the sale of electric energy generated at Bonneville Dam) would produce sufficient revenues to repay all reimbursable costs of Grand Coulee Dam, together with interest at 3 percent on the unamortized balance of investment allocated to power.

## Repayment Requirements

On November 28, 1945, a memorandum of understanding between the United States Army Engineers and the Bonneville Power Administration was executed, pursuant to the Bonneville Project Act, which provided, among other things, for repayment to the Treasury of capital costs of Bonneville Dam allocated to power. The memorandum provides that there shall be a "return to the Treasury of the capital costs allocable to power, including necessary additions and replacements, together with interest at 2.5 percent per annum on the unamortized investment and annual operating and maintenance expenses allocable to power" by the end of a 50-year period beginning July 1, 1944. There were substantial sales of electric energy generated at Bonneville Dam as early as 1940, and the project received the benefit of the application of net revenues (after provision for interest on the Federal investment allocated to power and exclusive of any provision for depreciation) of $1,831,323 toward debt amortization before the amortization period commenced on July 1, 1944.

The repayment reports of the Bonneville Power Administration indicate that the repayment requirements set forth above for Bonneville Dam have been assumed to apply also to the Bonneville-Grand Coulee transmission system, except that the required repayment period extends to the year 2001 (50 years from the proposed completion of these facilities in 1951).

On January 31, 1946, the Bureau of Reclamation and the Bonneville Power Administration executed a memorandum of understanding, pursuant to various statutes and to Executive Order No. 8526, referred to previously, providing, among other things, for the payment to the Bureau of Reclamation, from revenues received by the Bonneville Power Administration, of the following:

1. Operating and maintenance expenses and replacement costs, of joint and power facilities of the Columbia Basin project, not allocated to irrigation pumping power.

74

2. Construction costs of the project allocated to commercial power over periods of 50 years from July 1, 1942, for costs incurred prior to that date, and from the July 1 following the date put in operation for costs incurred subsequent to June 30, 1942.

3. Construction costs of the project allocated to down-stream river regulation over periods of 50 years from July 1 following substantial completion of power development to which allocated, and not later than June 30, 2017, for costs not reallocated to commercial power.

4. Construction costs of the project allocated to irrigation in excess of the finally determined repayment liability of water-users (estimated at $87,465,000) to be repaid as to each irrigation block within 50 years from the initial delivery of water, but the minimum repayment period for all such costs not to be less than 75 years from July 1, 1942.

5. Interest at 3 percent per annum on the unamortized balance of the commercial power allocation, including costs alocated to downstream river regulation from the time of reallocation to commercial power.

The foregoing payments to be subject to credit for miscellaneous revenues received by the project and for the excess of payments by water-users for power and energy used for irrigation pumping over operating expenses and replacement costs allocated to irrigation pumping power.

The entire reimbursable portions of the Federal investments in the Bonneville Power Administration and Bonneville Dam are to be repaid, with interest at 2½ percent from the time the investments are made, within periods of approximately 50 years. However, the repayment of Grand Coulee costs, while based upon computation of interest at the higher rate of 3 percent, does not include (1) any construction interest, (2) any interest on the excess of the reimbursable portion of the net investment over the unamortized cost incurred for facilities, (3) any interest on costs allocated to down-stream river regulation until such time as such costs may be reallocated to commercial power, or (4) any interest on the cost of irrigation facilities to be repaid from power revenues. Inasmuch as all construction costs (and some of the early operating costs) have been provided for by appropriations from general funds of the Treasury, all the above-mentioned interest costs represent additional subsidies which are not recognized in any of the reports on the project. The determination of the repayment requirements for the Columbia Basin project is based principally on the Reclamation Project Act of 1939 (the intent of which does not appear to be clear in this respect) and the interpretation of that law by a solicitor of the Department of the Interior (which has been seriously questioned—see quotation from House hearings on the Interior Department appropriation bill for 1949 elsewhere (p. 36) in this report). The cumulative amount of the above interest items omitted from construction costs and from repayments, based on a 2½ percent interest rate, is estimated to be in excess of $20,000,000 at June 30, 1947.

The repayment report of the Columbia River Power System as of June 30, 1947, contains repayment schedules based on the repayment requirements set forth in the afore-mentioned memorandums of understanding except that revenues have been allocated to all three projects in excess of such requirements. In order to compare the long-term investment in facilities at June 30, 1947, with the net revenues available for repayment thereof, the following adjustments were made:

1. Construction costs allocated to river regulation and irrigation which are to be repaid from power revenues were added to construction costs allocated to commercial power.

2. Expenditures for operation and maintenance and replacements, and interest expense on the debt to the Government, were excluded from the investment of the Government and from revenues.

3. Revenues not yet available for debt repayment, including accounts receivable and an advance to the Reclamation Fund for future operating expenses of the Columbia Basin project, were included in net revenues.

After applying the above adjustments, the construction costs to be repaid from power revenues, the net revenues available for such repayment, and the ratios of net revenues to construction costs, as of June 30, 1947, were determined to be as shown in the table on the opposite page.

| | Bonneville Dam project | Columbia Basin project[1] | Bonneville Power Administration | Total |
|---|---|---|---|---|
| Construction costs allocated to commercial power | $5, 8137, 933 | $97, 199, 949 | $97, 323, 575 | $252, 661, 457 |
| Other construction costs to be repaid by power: | | | | |
| Joint costs allocated to river regulation | | 30, 400, 395 | | 30, 400, 395 |
| Joint costs allocated to irrigation | | 59, 476, 049 | | 59, 476, 049 |
| 65.45 percent of construction cost of irrigation works (based on ratio to estimated total cost at 1945 prices of estimated portion thereof not recoverable from water users) | | 13, 999, 679 | | 13, 999, 679 |
| Total construction costs to be repaid from power revenues | 58, 137, 933 | 201, 076, 072 | 97, 323, 575 | 356, 537, 580 |
| Total receipts available for repayment | 18, 562, 150 | 28, 463, 968 | 50, 657, 297 | 97, 683, 415 |
| Less operation, maintenance, replacement, and interest expense repaid | 13, 423, 686 | 21, 158, 887 | 32, 856, 630 | 67, 439, 203 |
| Receipts available for repayment of construction costs | 5, 138, 464 | 7, 305, 081 | 17, 800, 667 | 30, 244, 212 |
| Add receivables, receipts in transit, and advance to reclamation fund for future expenses of Columbia Basin project | | | 6, 355, 327 | 6, 355, 327 |
| Total net revenues available for repayment of construction costs | 5, 138, 464 | 7, 305, 081 | 24, 155, 994 | 36, 599, 539 |
| Remainder of construction costs to be repaid from power revenues | 52, 999, 469 | 193, 770, 991 | 73, 167, 581 | 319, 938, 041 |
| Ratio of total net revenues to total construction costs | *Percent* 8. 84 | *Percent* 3. 63 | *Percent* 24. 82 | *Percent* 10. 27 |

[1] No construction interest is included on this project.

The 1947 repayment report indicates that at June 30, 1947, repayments were in excess of requirements by $152,282 for the Bonneville Dam project, $3,702,545 for the Columbia Basin project, and $10,182,-590 for Bonneville Power Administration. These amounts, which aggregate $14,037,417, appear to be correct on the basis of the requirements of the memorandums of understanding. However, proper interpretation of the meaning of these indicated excesses of actual repayments over required repayments requires consideration of the factors set forth in the two following paragraphs.

The Columbia Basin project is allowed a substantial advantage over the other two projects by reason of (1) not providing construction interest in the cost of facilities, (2) deferring interest on joint facilities allocated to river regulation and not providing any interest on joint facilities allocated to irrigation (all of which is to be repaid from power revenues) or on that portion of the cost of irrigation works to be repaid from power revenues, and (3) delaying amortization of the cost of joint facilities allocated to river regulation and irrigation, all of which cost is to be repaid from power revenues, even though these facilities are completed and in service. The repayment period for costs allocated to irrigation to be repaid from power revenues is set at 75 years, using 1940 prices for estimated total cost of irrigation works and making no provision for interest. If 1945 prices are used, the repayment period is extended another 11 years to 2028. If current prices were used the repayment period would have to be extended for an additional period beyond 86 years. If the Columbia Basin project had been required to make repayments on the same basis as the other two projects, by adding construction interest to the cost of all facilities to be repaid by power, and by paying interest, and currently repaying cost on that portion of facilities in service allocated to irrigation and river regulation which are to be repaid from power revenues, the combined excess of actual repayments over required repayments for all three projects would be substantially less. It is estimated that such additional repayment requirements would be in excess of $7,500,000 at June 30, 1947, and that in consequence the excess of repayments over requirements amounting to $14,037,417 (previously referred to) would be reduced to less than $6,500,000.

The repayment report of the Columbia River power system as of June 30, 1945, states that the estimated cost of irrigation works used in the Columbia Basin project repayment schedule is based on 1940 prices and that, if 1945 prices were used, such estimated costs would be increased by $74,561,820 and the repayment period would be extended to the year 2028, or 86 years from 1942. Although the estimated cost of the irrigation facilities had undoubtedly increased substantially over the 1945 estimate by June 30, 1947, the lower forecast, based on 1940 prices, was still used in the repayment schedule of the Columbia

Basin project at June 30, 1947. The failure to revise the estimated completed cost of irrigation works is based on the memorandum of understanding which provides that no change shall be made in the estimated completed costs of any facilities until completion or until actual expenditures exceed such estimates, and that if actual costs exceed estimates, recovery shall be made by extending the repayment period. Regardless of the provisions of the memorandum of understanding, the continued use of estimates based on 1940 prices is gravely misleading, in view of the fact that power revenues will be required to repay the entire increase in the cost of proposed irrigation works. In no place does the 1947 repayment report give any indication of the amount of the estimated additional cost of irrigation works which has been omitted from the repayment schedule.

## ANNUAL REPORTS

The annual reports of the Columbia River power system, beginning with the year ended June 30, 1945, have contained balance sheets and income statements for the individual projects, and combined balance sheets and income statements for the portion of the project allocated to power, which were examined and certified by independent public accountants. The presentation of the investment of the United States Government in these reports is considered open to criticism and subject to improvement in two respects, as set forth in the following paragraphs.

The statement of combined assets and liabilities allocated to power at June 30, 1947, shows the investment of the United States Government as follows:

| | |
|---|---:|
| Congressional appropriations, allotments, and WPA expenditures, less amounts not requisitioned | $310, 956, 764. 06 |
| Transfers from other Federal projects (net) | 1, 023, 661. 61 |
| Interest on Federal investment | 48, 149, 249. 89 |
| Total | 360, 129, 675. 56 |
| Less funds returned to U. S. Treasury in repayment of Federal investment | 99, 829, 217. 61 |
| Net investment of U. S. Government | 260, 300, 457. 95 |

The amount shown above for congressional appropriations, etc., includes approximately $34,000,000 appropriated for current operating expenses; the amount shown as interest on Federal investment includes approximately $33,400,000 of interest expense; and funds returned to the Treasury include repayments of such expenses and interest, approximately during the same periods in which the appropriations were withdrawn. The above presentation might lead the reader to conclude that the project had already repaid approximately 28 percent of the investment in the project, but this is true only on the as-

**79**

sumption used in the above presentation that appropriated funds used for current operating expenses represent an investment of the Government and that the reimbursement of those expenses to the Treasury from current revenues represents a repayment of the Government's investment. Such an assumption is not in conformity with the generally accepted business concept that the term "investment" in a business represents its capital or long-term advances or loans. If appropriations for, and repayments of, operation and maintenance expenses were excluded from the investment section of the balance sheet (as they are, for example, in the balance sheets of the Boulder Canyon project) the gross investment allocated to power would be reduced to approximately $292,700,000 (roughly equivalent to the original cost of facilities allocated to power) ; and repayments of investment allocated to power would be reduced to approximately $32,400,000, thereby indicating the actual repayment of approximately 11 percent of the investment allocable to power.

Power revenues are required to repay in addition to the investment allocated to power, as shown by the combined statement above, a substantial portion of the investment allocated to irrigation. At June 30, 1947, the investment allocated to irrigation, but to be repaid from power revenues, consisted of all joint construction costs allocated to irrigation, in the amount of $59,476,049 ; $13,999,679, representing approximately 65 percent (based on the ratios to estimated total construction costs at 1945 prices of the portion of those costs in excess of estimated collections from water users) of the construction costs of irrigation works incurred to June 30, 1947 ; and computed construction interest applicable to these two items in the amount of $5,727,803. Although these amounts, totaling $79,203,531, represent a long-term investment allocable to power for repayment, no indication of the fact appears in the financial statements or footnotes, and the entire amount is excluded from assets and investment in the combined balance sheet of assets and liabilities allocated to power. If the revised gross investment allocated to power of approximately $292,700,000 (shown in the preceding paragraph) were increased by this amount of $79,203,531, the indicated ratio of actual repayments to gross investment would be further reduced to approximately 9 percent.

In the foregoing computations, no amount is included as a charge against revenues for Federal, State, and local taxes which would be payable if the project were owned by private interests instead of by the Federal Government.

# Southwestern Power Administration

*(Department of the Interior)*

## How the Government Entered the Hydroelectric Power Business in the Southwest

The United States Government, acting through the Federal Emergency Administrator of Public Works, agreed by a contract dated October 16, 1937, with Grand River Dam Authority (a public corporation organized under the laws of the State of Oklahoma) to aid the Authority in financing the construction of a project on the Grand River in Oklahoma to provide water storage for the purpose of flood control and hydroelectric power development together with a hydroelectric generating plant and transmission lines.

The construction, operation, and maintenance of the original project by the Authority was authorized by a license effective January 1, 1939, issued by the Federal Power Commission.

In November 1941, by Executive Order No. 8944, the Grand River dam project, then under construction, was taken over by the Government from the Grand River Dam Authority, pursuant to section 16 of the Federal Power Act, to be completed and operated by the Government during the war emergency. Government operation of the project was carried on under the Federal Works Agency from November 1941 until September 1, 1943, at which time this function was transferred to the Department of the Interior by Executive Order No. 9373.

Meanwhile, under the provisions of the Flood Control Act of 1938, construction was started in 1939 on the Denison dam project on the Red River in Texas and Oklahoma, and on the Norfork dam project located on the North Fork River in Arkansas. Both projects were constructed by the War Department under the supervision of the United States Army Corps of Engineers for the combined purposes of flood control and production of hydroelectric power and were placed in operation by the War Department, under the supervision of the United States Army Corps of Engineers, in June 1944. Under the Executive orders referred to, the Secretary of the Interior became the agent of the Government for the sale of electric energy produced from these three projects.

## The Southwestern Power Administration and Its Functions

On August 31, 1943, the Secretary of the Interior issued Departmental Order No. 1865, creating and designating the Southwestern

Power Administration to perform his functions under authority granted by Executive Order No. 9373. This order charged the Secretary of the Interior with the responsibility, among other things, of selling the electric energy generated at the Denison, Norfork, and Grand River dam projects to war plants, public bodies and cooperatives, and other persons, in that order of preference, at rates approved by the Federal Power Commission. This order also transferred to the Secretary of the Interior all property of the Grand River Dam Authority, theretofore under control of the Federal Works Administrator by authority of Executive Order No. 8944, dated November 19, 1941.

The Flood Control Act of December 1944, which authorized the construction of a number of dams for flood control and other purposes, provided in section 5 for the transmission and disposal of electric power and energy from such projects, as follows:

SECTION 5. Electric power and energy generated at reservoir projects under the control of the War Department and in the opinion of the Secretary of War not required in the operation of such projects shall be delivered to the Secretary of the Interior, who shall transmit and dispose of such power and energy in such manner as to encourage the most widespread use thereof at the lowest possible rates to consumers consistent with sound business principles, the rate schedules to become effective upon confirmation and approval by the Federal Power Commission. Rate schedules shall be drawn having regard to the recovery (upon the basis of the application of such rate schedules to the capacity of the electric facilities of the projects) of the cost of producing and transmitting such electric energy, including the amortization of the capital investment allocated to power over a reasonable period of years. Preference in the sale of such power and energy shall be given to public bodies and cooperatives. The Secretary of the Interior is authorized, from funds to be appropriated by the Congress, to construct or acquire, by purchase or other agreement, only such transmission lines and related facilities as may be necessary in order to make the power and energy generated at said projects available at wholesale quantities for sale on fair and reasonable terms and conditions to facilities owned by the Federal Government, public bodies, cooperatives, and privately owned companies. All moneys received from such sales shall be deposited in the treasury of the United States as miscellaneous receipts.

PROJECTS COMPRISING THE SOUTHWESTERN POWER ADMINISTRATION, THEIR LOCATION, CONSTRUCTION, AND OPERATION

The area in which the Southwestern Power Administration operates comprises the States of Louisiana, Arkansas, and that part of Missouri and Kansas south of the Missouri River Basin and east of the ninety-eighth meridian, and that part of Oklahoma and Texas lying east of the ninety-ninth meridian and north of the San Antonio River Basin. These boundaries were established by Interior Department Order No. 2135, dated November 21, 1945.

With the exception of the Grand River dam project (which was returned to the Grand River Dam Authority under agreement dated

August 1, 1946), construction and operation of hydroelectric projects in this system are performed by the Corps of Engineers, Department of the Army.

At June 30, 1947, the Corps of Engineers, Department of the Army, had substantially completed the construction of hydroelectric generating facilities at the Denison and Norfork projects (each of 35,000 kilowatt capacity) at a recorded cost of $79,591,845. Twenty-two other projects have been authorized, of which 10 were under construction at June 30, 1947, their recorded cost at that date being $12,351,332. Available estimates at June 30, 1947, indicate that the ultimate cost of all authorized projects will aggregate approximately $730,907,000. It has been estimated that the ultimate generating capacities of all projects (including 10 proposed projects not yet authorized, and not mentioned above) will be approximately 1,917,000 kilowatts.

## DISTRIBUTING AND MARKETING OF HYDROELECTRIC ENERGY

The disposal of the electric power output of the Federally owned Denison and Norfork projects has been accomplished by the Administration by selling at the bus bar, using existing transmission facilities of private utilities companies situated in the area. Section 5 of the Flood Control Act of December 1944, authorizes the Secretary of the Interior to construct or otherwise acquire only such transmission lines and related facilities as may be necessary to make power and energy generated at the projects available to consumers.

For the purpose of construction and acquisition of transmission lines, substations, and appurtenant facilities, and expenses connected therewith, the Congress appropriated $7,500,000 for the fiscal year 1947. At the close of that year, $509,419 had been spent on transmission facilities as reported in monthly financial statements issued by the Administration. This amount includes no provision for interest during construction which at June 30, 1947, amounted to $6,368, computed for one-half year at the rate of 2½ percent per annum on the total in the construction account at that date.

## OPERATION, MAINTENANCE, AND CARE

The financial reports of the Southwestern Power Administration show that during the four years ended June 30, 1947, expenses for marketing of power and energy generated at the Norfork and Denison projects amounted to $339,042. Congressional appropriations for this purpose were as follows:

| | |
|---|---|
| 1945 | $135,000 |
| 1946 | 140,000 |
| 1947 | 110,000 |
| 1944 | 100,000 |
| Total | 485,000 |

Revenues from sale of power and energy generated at the projects during these periods aggregated $3,355,203 an dhave been deposited by the Administration in the Treasury of the United States as miscellaneous receipts, as required by section 5 of the Flood Control Act of December 1944. The Denison and Norfolk projects were first put into service on a testing basis in June 1944 and continued in that manner until March 1945, at which time, the administrator reported, production had reached commercial proportions.

Expenses of the Corps of Engineers charged to the operation and maintenance of these two projects aggregated $1,205,107 to June 30, 1947. Deduction of this amount, and of the amount of $339,042 previously mentioned, from gross revenues shows net revenues (before provision for replacements) of $1,811,054.

## AMORTIZATION OF CONSTRUCTION COST AND REPAYMENT OF OPERATING EXPENSES

The projects of the Southwestern Power Administration are what are commonly referred to as multiple-purpose projects. From the dams, reservoirs and other installations, benefits may accrue jointly to flood control, power, navigation, or river regulation. Other facilities, such as electric power plants and transmission lines, are constructed specifically for power generation and transmission, and benefits to other features from this source may be very limited. Because certain facilities serve both power and other uses, it is customary to make allocations of the costs of joint facilities among power and other than power features.

At June 30, 1947, a basis for allocating the construction costs of projects with which the Southwestern Power Administration is concerned had not been agreed upon. Although the Corps of Engineers had tentatively allocated to power $24,534,488 of Denison and Norfolk construction costs, the administrator of the Southwestern Power Administration made the following statements which are published in hearings before the Subcommittee of the Committee on Appropriations, House of Representatives, Eightieth Congress, second session, Interior Department appropriation bill for 1949:

There have been no final allocations made. I wish there was some way of making an allocation in advance, and I hope some day at least there is developed a system by which they allocate these things as they build them, when people know what the costs are.

When you go around and try to find out, after they are finished, or try to find out where certain money went for construction, it is quite a job, but we are working on it now.

There has been a tentative allocation nobody accepts as final, and we will not put in any financial statement, as I told the committee last year, any tentative allocation which will change the picture later on. We are not going to tell the Congress one thing and then 5 years later say we have to make a restudy.

There may be some benefit from the set-up to navigation, but the allocation will have everything used for power, I believe in a conservative way. If there is any question about it, I think power ought to do the job.

Mr. Chairman, I want the committee to understand exactly what we are doing and how we are doing these things. There is nothing which is iron-bound. The Army, the Federal Power Commission, and Southwestern all have a definite stake in this allocation.

Frankly, I don't think any one of the three of us would completely trust the other in making an allocation, and that may be good. There are three of us making it together, and if the Army finds from their viewpoint of flood control that such is the situation, they have to justify it to Congress in order to get the proper appropriations, and we say that power is paramount, and frankly I want power to pay every bit of the cost. Then I will make a statement which may surprise you. It is going to take us some time to make these allocations. Some of them have not been made for 10 years after the projects were completed. * * *

In making the computations for amortization requirements and available revenues, it was assumed that power revenues will be required to repay the entire project construction cost on an equal-annual-payment basis with interest compounded at 2½ percent per annum over a period of 50 years, beginning July 1, 1945. The Federal Power Commission, in its Administrative Memorandum No. 12, has stated that the replacement requirements of Federally owned hydroelectric projects average approximately 0.6 percent of the completed project construction cost on a sinking fund basis. Accordingly, in making the computations, effect has been given to such provisions for replacements at 0.6 percent, with interest at 2½ percent per annum

On the basis just described, and including interest during construction, the total investment to June 30, 1947 was $82,927,368. No allocations of costs have been made (as stated above) though it is indicated that some portion of the total costs may be allocated to flood control, navigation and river regulation. In the absence of such allocations, our computation is made on the basis that all costs will be repaid from power revenues.

The income available for such purposes in 1947 was $374,407, or less than one half of 1 percent of the total investment. The total income required for that year to amortize the investment in equal annual payments in 50 years with 2½ percent interest compounded annually is $2,871,570.

The cumulative results to June 30, 1947 are as follows:

| | |
|---|---:|
| Payments required on the above basis | $8,431,900 |
| Total credit with Treasury available for repayment | 398,804 |
| Deficiency | 8,033,096 |
| Add 2½ percent interest on deficiency at the close of each fiscal year | 216,064 |
| Cumulative excess of required annual payments over available credit with Treasury | 8,249,160 |

Following is a reconcilement of the net power revenues before provision for replacements with the credit available with the Treasury for repayment of construction costs:

Net revenue (before provision for replacements)_____ $1, 811, 054

Add:

    One-half year's interest at 2½ percent on annual net cash revenues available for payment into the Treasury_____ 22, 641

    Interest at 2½ percent on the cumulative balance of provisions for replacements_____ 35, 455

    Total_____ 1, 869, 150

Deduct provision for replacements on basis of Federal Power Commission Administrative Memorandum No. 12 (0.6 percent)_____ 1, 470, 346

    Total credit with Treasury available for repayment_____ 398, 804

## SCOPE OF OUR SURVEY

Our report has been compiled from information contained in various published reports, documents, and hearings, and from information available from financial reports and statements compiled by the Southwestern Power Administration and the Corps of Engineers. The element of interest during construction and the 0.6 percent provision for replacement were computed by us, as no such provisions had been included in those financial reports and statements.

From information contained in numerous reports, many assumptions could be made and various methods devised to show the ability of the projects to produce sufficient revenues to repay the Federal investment, with interest, over a reasonable period of years as prescribed in section 5 of the Flood Control Act of 1944. However, such repayment ability is not only governed by the maximum amount of revenue that the projects may be estimated to produce, but is dependent to an even greater degree on the amount of construction costs allocated to reimbursable features of the projects. It follows, therefore, that any portion of construction cost allocated to the nonreimbursable features represents a Government subsidy and reduces the repayment requirements.

In the absence of any allocations of costs, we have had to assume that all costs will be repaid from power revenues. On this basis, we find that, as stated above, the revenues fall far short of meeting the annual amortization requirements, and, in 1947, were less than one-half of 1 percent of the total investment (income available $374,407; total investment $82,927,368). Furthermore, in another year or two a portion of the annual revenue will be required for amortization of transmission facilities now under construction by the Administration, for which the Congress appropriated $7,500,000 in 1947.

The second 35,000-kilowatt generating units are now in process of being installed at each of the two projects but we were informed that at June 30, 1948, these new units had not been put into service. Even with the new units in service (which would increase the productive capacity of each of the two projects to 70,000 kilowatts) prospective revenues at present rates would still fall far short of meeting annual amortization requirements on the basis used above.

We were informed that no commercial type audit of the accounts of the Administration has ever been made and that no legal authority exists for the employment of outside accountants for that purpose. It is stated, however, that during the fiscal year ended June 30, 1948, the accounts were examined by members of the House Investigating Committee on Appropriations.

It has been asserted by private public utilities interests that Southwestern Power Administration is engaged in, or plans to engage in, extensive duplication of existing transmission facilities. We do not express an opinion as to the merits of this contention.

In the foregoing computations, no amount is included as a charge against revenues for Federal, State, and local taxes which would be payable if the project were owned by private interests instead of by the Federal Government.

# Tennessee Valley Authority

The Tennessee Valley Authority was created by an act of Congress approved May 18, 1933, for the purposes of improving navigability and providing for flood control of the Tennessee River, providing for reforestation and the proper use of marginal lands in the Tennessee Valley, providing for the agricultural and industrial development of the Tennessee Valley, providing for the national defense, and for other purposes.

The Tennessee Valley Authority is a corporation without capital stock managed by a board of three directors who are appointed by the President with the advice and consent of the Senate. It was financed by an allocation of $50,000,000 from the National Industrial Recovery Appropriation of 1933, an allocation of $25,000,000 from the Emergency Appropriation Act of 1935, subsequent appropriations from general funds of the Treasury, and revenues from power and other operations.

Wilson Dam, nitrate and stream plants at Sheffield and Muscle Shoals, Ala., and other associated properties, formerly under the jurisdiction of the War Department, were turned over to the Authority at its inception, for the production and sale of power and the development of commercial fertilizer.

Under the original act and subsequent amendments, the Authority was given, among others, the following corporate powers:

1. The right to sue and be sued.
2. The right to make certain contracts.
3. The right to purchase or lease real and personal property.
4. The power to exercise the right of eminent domain.
5. The power to construct and to acquire real estate for the construction of dams, reservoirs, transmission lines, powerhouses, and other structures, and navigation projects along the Tennessee River and any of its tributaries.
6. The power to advise and cooperate in the readjustment of the population displaced by construction or acquisition of dams, reservoir areas, etc.
7. Various powers in connection with the experimental development, production, and sale of experimental fertilizers and the production of certain materials for military purposes.
8. The authority to produce, distribute, and sell electric power.

The specified duties of the Authority include the following:

1. To file annually with the President and with the Congress a financial statement and report covering each fiscal year.
2. To operate the dams and reservoirs primarily for the purposes of promoting navigation and controlling floods and, consistent with such purposes, to produce

and sell electric energy in order to avoid the waste of water power and to assist in liquidating the cost of the projects. Preference in the sale of power is required to be given to States, counties, municipalities, and cooperative organizations.

3. To make payments to States and counties in lieu of taxes, at rates gradually decreasing from 10 percent (in the fiscal year beginning July 1, 1940) to 5 percent (in the fiscal year beginning July 1, 1948, and thereafter) of the gross revenues from the sale of power to customers other than agencies and departments of the Federal Government.

Under an act of Congress, approved February 24, 1945, and under the Government Corporation Control Act, approved December 6, 1945, the Authority has had annual business-type audits, beginning with the year ended June 30, 1945, by the Corporation Audits Division of the General Accounting Office. Prior to the fiscal year 1942 there was disagreement as to whether the Authority was subject to the usual voucher-type audit by the General Accounting Office and no final audit reports were issued by the General Accounting Office. An amendment to the act in November 1941 provided that, notwithstanding the provisions of any other law governing the expenditure of public funds, the General Accounting Office should not disallow credit for any disbursements which the board of directors (of the Authority) determines to have been necessary to carry out the provisions of the act.

The management of the Authority has interpreted its powers to include the right to retain surplus revenues and to expend such revenues for the completion of authorized projects and for the extension of transmission lines and other purposes.

At June 30, 1947, 16 multiple-use dams, 12 single-use (for power) dams, 10 steam plants, and extensive transmission, navigation, and chemical facilities had been constructed, purchased from private utilities companies, or acquired from other departments or agencies of the Government, and 2 major multiple-use dams were under construction. The generating capacity of the system at June 30, 1947, was 2,538,902 kilowatts and 402,600 kilowatts of additional capacity were under construction.

APPROPRIATIONS

As of June 30, 1947, Government funds made available from new appropriations (including $65,072,500 from the sale of bonds to the Treasury and the Reconstruction Finance Corporation and $75,000,000 from emergency appropriations) and the assigned value of properties transferred from other Government departments and agencies totaled $822,831,346. Of this amount, $33,883,322 represented unused appropriations. In addition to the new appropriations, proceeds from the sale of bonds, and properties transferred to the Authority, the Authority had retained, as working capital or for reinvestment in facilities, revenues totaling approximately $131,692,600. This latter amount

**89**

represents the excess of net power revenues before provisions for depreciation and for amortization of acquisition cost adjustments, $155,-324,119, over repayments to the Treasury (exclusive of interest on bonded indebtedness) of $23,631,519, the latter amount consisting of $8,572,500 of bonds retired and $15,059,019 of repayments to the Government on its investment in power facilities. Further reference to this subject is made later in this report under the heading "Repayment requirements."

During the fiscal year 1939, the Authority issued 2⅛ percent and 2½ percent bonds in the face amount of $8,572,500, which were purchased by the Reconstruction Finance Corporation and the United States Treasury. These bonds had all been redeemed by June 30, 1947. Under authority granted by an amendment to the act in 1939, the Authority issued, during the fiscal years 1940 and 1941, $56,500,000 of 1¾ percent to 2½ percent serial bonds, the proceeds of which were used principally in the acquisition of existing power properties from private utilities companies. These bonds were all purchased by the United States Treasury and, by agreement, the interest rate was reduced to ½ percent for 1940 and 1941 and 1 percent thereafter. At June 30, 1947, the entire amount of $56,500,000 was still outstanding.

ALLOCATION OF COSTS

The board of directors is required to determine, and file annually (whenever additional properties have been completed) with the Congress, allocations to the various purposes of the value of all properties serving more than one of the purposes for which the Authority was created. The total amount of such joint costs so allocated as of June 30, 1947, was $352,181,452, which was less than half of the Government's total investment in Tennessee Valley Authority. These joint costs were allocated as follows:

| | |
|---|---|
| Power (40 percent) | $140, 872, 581 |
| Navigation (30 percent) | 105, 654, 435 |
| Flood control (30 percent) | 105, 654, 436 |
| Total | 352 ,181, 452 |

The recommendations of the General Accounting Office, with respect to the Authority, as included in the House hearings on the Government corporations appropriation bill for 1949, state that insufficient costs may have been allocated to power and that a new determination of the allocation of the cost of multiple-use facilities is needed. Following is an extract from these recommendations:

On the basis of our review of the Authority's evaluation of the navigation and flood-control-tangible benefits, the portion of the cost of multiple-use facilities allocated by the Board to the two purposes is not justified.

90

At June 30, 1947, the cost of facilities allocated to programs other than power, exclusive of interest during construction, amounted to approximately $348,425,000, working capital allocated to programs other than power amounted to approximately $25,767,000, and the accumulated net expense of such programs, before provisions for depreciation, amounted to approximately $64,247,000. These costs are nonreimbursable except for revenues from the sale of fertilizer, receipts from the sale of property, and other miscellaneous income. At June 30, 1947, $7,874,989, derived from such sources, had been repaid to the Treasury.

REPAYMENT REQUIREMENTS

The Tennessee Valley Authority Act, as amended, declared it to be the policy of the act that:

* * * in order, as soon as practicable, to make the power projects self-supporting and self-liquidating, the surplus power shall be sold at rates which, in the opinion of the Board, when applied to the normal capacity of the Authority's power facilities, will produce gross revenues in excess of the cost of production of said power. * * *

Facilities constructed by the Authority are carried on the books at cost, except that interest during construction is not included. Completed facilities acquired by purchase are carried on the books at original cost and accrued depreciation at dates of acquisition is credited to the reserves for depreciation. Of the net excess of purchase cost over net book value at dates of acquisition (original cost less accrued depreciation) in the amount of $9,502,032, all of which is allocated to power, $8,324,153 had been charged against power revenues at June 30, 1947, leaving an unamortized balance of $1,177,879.

Section 26 of the act gave the Board unusual control over revenues in that it exempted from the general provision that all proceeds from the sale of power or other products and from the sale of real or personal property must be deposited in the Treasury, "such part of such proceeds as in the opinion of the Board shall be necessary for the Corporation in the operation of dams and reservoirs, in conducting its business in generating, transmitting, and distributing electric energy and in manufacturing, selling, and distributing fertilizer and fertilizer ingredients. A continuing fund of $1,000,000 is also excepted * * *." Under this provision, the Authority retained all revenues from power operations through June 30, 1944, except for the retirement of bonds in the principal amount of $2,000,000. Additional bonds in the principal amount of $6,372,500 were retired during the 3 years ended June 30, 1947. During the fiscal years 1946 and 1947, the Authority also repaid to the Treasury $22,934,008, of which $15,059,019 was determined by the Authority to represent repayments of the Government's investment in power facilities, the remainder of $7,874,989 (referred to above) being allocable to other programs.

Repayment requirements were amended, and the freedom to reinvest power revenues was curtailed, by certain provisions of the Government Corporations Appropriation Act, 1948, approved July 30, 1947. These provisions require the repayment from power revenues of a total amount of $348,239,240 during the 40-year period beginning July 1, 1947, at least one-fourth of which amount shall be paid in each 10-year period; the repayments during the years ending June 30, 1948, and 1949 are required to be at least $10,500,000 and $5,500,000, respectively; and the required repayments as stated above are to include at least $2,500,000 annually for the retirement of bonds. Provision is also made for the repayment of all additional appropriations for power facilities (beginning with appropriations for the fiscal year 1948) over a period not in excess of 40 years after the year in which the facilities are placed in operation. This act further provides that:

None of the power revenues of the Tennessee Valley Authority shall be used for the construction of new power producing projects (except for replacement purposes) unless and until approved by act of Congress.

The amount of $348,239,240 is the approximate excess of the sum of (1) the gross investment in facilities allocated to power at June 30, 1947, (2) the net cost of retirements to that date, and (3) the cash on hand, inventories, and receivables allocated to power at that date, over the sum of the net power revenues to June 30, 1947, and the provisions for depreciation and for amortization of acquisition adjustments. No provision is made for repayment of interest during construction of the facilities or for payment of interest on the balance still to be repaid. However, in conformity with our standard procedure in reviewing the ability of all Government power projects to repay costs, and in view of published statements made in connection with the original publication of TVA power rates to the effect that it was the intention "that the rates would be sufficient to pay interest on the entire debt" and that "the project was designed to be strictly self-supporting and self-liquidating," we have, in our determination of computed repayment requirements, included interest during construction at 3 percent and interest at 3 percent annually on the unpaid balance of the debt representing the cost of completed facilities allocated to power.

Inasmuch as no revision of repayment requirements was made prior to the Government Corporations Appropriation Act, 1948, it may be assumed that the Authority's practice of retaining the greater part of its net power revenues (before provision for depreciation) for reinvestment met with the approval of the Congress. Therefore, in view of the basis used in that act to determine the amount to be repaid, the repayment tests made in connection with this report have been made on the assumption that the net power revenues retained by the Authority were, in effect, returned to the Treasury in repayment of the debt and reappropriated by the Congress.

In order to apply our standard repayment test to facilities allocated to power, on the basis of equal annual payments over 50-year periods, with interest at 3 percent, compounded annually, it was necessary to make certain adjustments to the cost of these facilities as reported in the Authority's annual published reports. Reported cost of completed facilities allocated to power at the close of each fiscal year (including unamortized acquisition cost adjustments) was reduced by that amount which was offset by depreciation reserves at dates of acquisition and increased by the accumulated amortization of acquisition cost adjustments and by construction interest computed at 3 percent for the periods from average dates of expenditure to the beginning of the fiscal year following completion. The resulting cost of facilities allocated to power at June 30, 1947, including construction interest of $21,992,707, amounted to $493,537,933, of which $468,174,004 represented facilities in service and $25,363,929 represented construction in progress.

The reported net power revenues were also adjusted, for purposes of testing the extent to which the power operations were meeting repayment requirements under the 50-year equal-annual-payment plan. The approximate required provisions for replacements were computed by applying to original cost as recorded, increased by computed construction interest and the acquisition cost adjustments referred to above, the rates set forth for Federal hydroelectric projects in the Federal Power Commission's Administrative Memorandum No. 12. No recognition was given to the net expenses of non-income-producing programs, which expenses are shown by the Authority's financial statements to aggregate $92,497,057 at June 30, 1947. In order to determine the annual computed credit available with the Treasury for repayment of the cost of facilities allocated to power, the reported net power revenues of $92,566,675 were adjusted as follows:

Additions to net power revenues:

| | |
|---|---:|
| Provisions for depreciation and for amortization of acquisition adjustments (noncash expenses) | $62,772,389 |
| Interest paid to Reconstruction Finance Corporation and U. S. Treasury on bonded indebtedness | 5,224,700 |
| ½ year's interest at 3 percent on estimated net cash revenues (as hereby adjusted) available for payment into the Treasury | 2,225,844 |
| Interest at 3 percent on the cumulative balance of computed additional provisions for replacements | 295,882 |
| Total additions to net power revenues | 70,518,815 |

**93**

Deductions from net power revenues:

Net cost of retirements, taken as a measure of the cost of replacements incurred_____ $12, 174, 103

Computed additional required provision for replacements (the excess of total computed required provision over the net cost of retirements)_____ 5, 055, 987

Total deductions from net power revenues_____ 17, 230, 090

Net additions to net power revenues_____ 53, 288, 725
Net power revenues as reported_____ 92, 566, 675

Total—accumulated computed net credits available for repayments_____ 145, 855, 400

Comparison of the foregoing with the annual repayment requirements, on the basis of equal annual payments over periods of 50 years following completion, with interest at 3 percent compounded annually (computed on the debt basis set forth above), shows that by June 30, 1947, the accumulated computed net credits available for repayment ($145,855,400), exceeded the accumulated requirements by $47,060,917. It is therefore apparent that, on the basis of the recorded allocation of joint costs among power and nonreimbursable purposes (as to the propriety of which we express no opinion), the power revenues are well in excess of those required to repay over 50-year periods the cost of facilities allocated to power, even when construction interest is included in the cost of facilities, and interest is charged at 3 percent on the unpaid debt balance.

The comparison of assumed annual computed net credits available with the Treasury for repayment with the computed annual repayment requirements (both computed on the bases set forth in preceding paragraphs) is as follows:

| Period | Computed net credit available with the Treasury | Computed repayment requirement | Surplus (deficiency) |
|---|---|---|---|
| Year ended June 30: | | | |
| 1934_____ | $480, 133 | $734, 511 | $( 254, 378) |
| 1935_____ | (14, 551) | 735, 076 | (749, 627) |
| 1936_____ | 231, 669 | 812, 136 | (580, 467) |
| 1937_____ | 746, 685 | 893, 522 | (146, 837) |
| 1938_____ | 688, 511 | 2, 417, 017 | (1, 728, 506) |
| 1939_____ | 2, 826, 869 | 3, 216, 565 | (389, 696) |
| 1940_____ | 7, 857, 038 | 3, 684, 457 | 4, 172, 581 |
| 1941_____ | 10, 964, 037 | 7, 400, 120 | 3, 563, 917 |
| 1942_____ | 8, 416, 839 | 7, 816, 472 | 600, 367 |
| 1943_____ | 18, 333, 522 | 10, 124, 640 | 8, 208, 882 |
| 1944_____ | 19, 950, 887 | 11, 791, 125 | 8, 159, 762 |
| 1945_____ | 24, 556, 272 | 13, 875, 068 | 10, 681, 204 |
| 1946_____ | 22, 877, 995 | 17, 413, 077 | 5, 464, 918 |
| 1947_____ | 27, 939, 494 | 17, 880, 697 | 10, 058, 797 |
| Total_____ | 145, 855, 400 | 98, 794, 483 | 47, 060, 917 |

The excess of the computed credit available with the Treasury for repayment over the computed repayment requirement, for the year ended June 30, 1947, is $10,058,797, computed as follows:

Computed credit available with the Treasury for the year ended June 30, 1947:

| | |
|---|---:|
| Reported net power revenues | $21,248,377 |
| Add: | |
| Provision for depreciation allocated to power | 8,516,410 |
| Provision for amortization of acquisition adjustments | 200,000 |
| Interest paid on bonds | 615,570 |
| Total | 30,580,357 |
| Less net cost of retirements allocated to power | 1,586,618 |
| Remainder—estimated net cash revenues available for payment to the Treasury | 28,993,739 |
| Add interest at 3 percent for average period of ½ year | 434,906 |
| Total | 29,428,645 |
| Less computed additional required provision for replacements | 1,593,039 |
| Remainder | 27,835,606 |
| Add interest on cumulative excess of computed required provision for replacements over net cost of retirements (3 percent of $3,462,948) | 103,888 |
| Total—computed credit available with the Treasury for repayment | 27,939,494 |

Less computed repayment requirement for the year ended June 30, 1947 (based on cost of completed facilities at June 30, 1946):

| | | |
|---|---:|---:|
| Reported original cost: | | |
| Multiple-use dams allocated to power | $273,251,512 | |
| Single-use (power) dams | 46,512,554 | |
| Steam production plants | 29,041,066 | |
| Other electric plant | 103,818,183 | |
| Total original cost of facilities allocated to power | 452,623,315 | |
| Add: | | |
| Unamortized acquisition adjustments | 1,377,879 | |
| Accumulated amortization of acquisition adjustments | 8,124,153 | |
| Total | 462,125,347 | |
| Less accrued depreciation at dates acquired | 22,706,525 | |
| Remainder—cost to TVA | 439,418,822 | |
| Add computed 3 percent interest during construction | 20,647,219 | |
| Cost to TVA, including interest during construction | 460,066,041 | |
| Equal annual payment required to amortize in 50 years, with interest at 3 percent compounded annually (3.88655 percent of $460,066,041) | | 17,880,697 |
| Remainder—excess of computed credit available with the Treasury for repayment over computed repayment requirement | | 10,058,797 |

**95**

If the computed credit available with the Treasury for repayment in each year is reduced by interest at 3 percent on the unpaid balance of the cost of completed facilities allocated to power at the beginning of that year, and the remainder applied to reduce such unpaid balance for succeeding years (any excess of interest over credit being added to the unpaid balance for succeeding years), the balance of the debt applicable to completed facilities allocated to power at June 30, 1947, is computed to be $393,261,454. Repayment of this amount in equal annual payments over the 40-year period specified in the Government Corporations Appropriation Act, 1948, but with interest at 3 percent, compounded annually, would require 40 payments of $17,013,426, or a total of $680,537,058. This latter amount exceeds the repayments of $348,239,240 required by that act, by $332,297,818.

It should be noted that the debt allocated to power for the repayment computations in the preceding paragraph does not include (1) construction in progress allocated to power at June 30, 1947, in an estimated amount of $24,239,374, (2) estimated construction interest thereon in the amount of $1,124,555, or (3) cash, receivables, and inventories allocated to power as shown by the published annual report for the year ended June 30, 1947, in the amount of $24,531,115. In making the above computations relative to repayments, no charge has been computed for interest on working capital allocable to power.

RECOMMENDATIONS

While the computations reviewed above indicate that the Authority is presently earning more than sufficient revenues from power operations to repay the investment in power facilities, with interest, we recommend that the Congress reconsider the requirements for repayment as specified in the Government Corporations Appropriation Act of 1948 in view of the intent stated in the act "to make the power projects self-supporting and self-liquidating" and in particular that it determine (1) whether TVA should not pay into the Treasury all of its net income, or (2) whether the repayments should not be increased so as to be sufficient to repay the investment in 50 years with interest at 3 percent. In the latter case, while the amounts so required to be repaid would be almost double the present requirement, the earnings on the basis of 1947 results would be more than sufficient for that purpose. In either case, the computations of the amount to be repaid should provide for construction interest and also for interest on the unpaid balance of the debt allocable to completed power facilities.

It is also recommended that all new construction be authorized by the Congress; that new appropriations be made therefor; and that the Authority not be permitted to construct new facilities with its power revenues, except in case of unforeseen emergencies as to which the fund of $1,000,000 is available and with respect to which subsequent approval could be obtained from the Congress. Under the present law the restriction on the reinvestment of power revenues applies only to new power-producing projects and therefore permits the use of power revenues for the construction of new transmission facilities and might be interpreted to permit the use of such revenues for the construction of new generating facilities.

The other recommendations set forth in our introductory statement, where not already in effect, should be considered as applying to the Tennessee Valley Authority.

## Taxes

As previously stated, the Authority is required to make payments to States and counties in lieu of taxes at rates gradually decreasing from 10 percent (in the fiscal year beginning July 1) to 5 percent (in the fiscal year beginning July 1, 1948, and thereafter) of the gross revenues from the sale of power to customers other than agencies and departments of the Federal Government. By comparison, the Federal Power Commission has reported for the year 1946 that Federal, State, and local taxes for all class A and B utilities in the United States averaged 19 percent of gross revenues, or 5 percent of gross plant investment.

## General

The published annual reports of the Authority were found to be comprehensive and to present clearly the financial condition of the Authority and the results of its operations. The report on the audit of the Authority for the fiscal year ended June 30, 1945, by the Corporation Audits Division of the General Accounting Office, stated as follows:

In our opinion, TVA's accounts generally were well conceived, supervised, and maintained, and the Authority is to be commended as one of the foremost Government corporations in the use of accounting in management, comparing quite favorably in this respect with well-managed private corporations.

# APPENDIX TO PARTS I, II, AND III

## Examples of Misleading Presentations of Financial Data, Lack of Consistency in Reporting, and Information Contained in Records of Congressional Hearings Which Is Not Factual

REPORTS OF THE DEVELOPMENT OF WATER RESOURCES OF RIVER BASINS

Reference is made to the following elaborate reports prepared by the Bureau of Reclamation:

The Colorado River, March 1946, 293 pages.

The Columbia River, February 1947, 393 pages.

Missouri River Basin, April 1944, 211 pages.

In each of these reports the impression seems to be given that the projects are to pay interest at 3 percent and to amortize the investment in 50 years. A study of the portion of the report concerned with economic feasibility demonstrates, however, that it is not the intention to make provision for interest.

The showing as to economic feasibility is in two parts:

(*a*) A comparison of annual benefits with annual costs.

(*b*) A comparison of total revenues for 50 years with estimated cost of investment (1940 prices).

By way of example this summary is quoted from the report on the Colorado River:

*Annual Benefits*

| | |
|---|---|
| Irrigation benefits | $65, 000, 000 |
| Power benefits | 72, 000, 000 |
| Flood-control benefits | 1, 000, 000 |
| Municipal benefits | 500, 000 |
| Total measurable annual benefits | 138, 500, 000 |

*Annual Costs*

| | |
|---|---|
| Operation and maintenance | 23, 000, 000 |
| Amortization of construction cost ($2,185,442,000) in 50 years at 3 percent | 85, 000, 000 |
| Total annual costs | 108, 000, 000 |

*Ratio of Benefits to Costs*

| | |
|---|---|
| Ration of annual benefits to annual costs | 1.3 : 1 |

The item of $85,000,000 is correctly computed as the equal annual payment required to amortize the total investment of $2,185,442,000

98

(of which, it is stated, $25,000,000 may reasonably be allocated to flood control) in 50 years with interest at 3 percent compounded annually. At this point there appears to be at least an intention to provide for amortization and interest. However, the only cash revenues expected to be available to meet the total annual costs of $108,000,000 are the revenue from power of $72,000,000, collections from water users of $8,000,000, and returns of $500,000 from the sale of water for municipal purposes. The other substantial item in the benefits is irrigation benefits of $65,000,000, which is the estimated increase in gross farm income resulting from irrigation. However, the report estimates that only $8,000,000 could be paid by the water users (farmers) annually, which is the only amount in respect to irrigation that will be available to meet the annual costs.

In all three reports the costs of operations are based on 1940 prices, as are the estimates of construction costs. (The revised draft plan of Columbia River Basin, dated February 1947, also gives tables of costs and benefits on the basis of 1946 prices.)

The second step in the justification for Colorado River, namely, comparison of total revenues with estimated cost of investment (at 1940 prices) is accomplished by a statement that gross revenues will amount to $57,500,000 annually in excess of costs for operation and maintenance. This means that net revenues will be short, $27,500,000 annually, of earning the amount of amortization and interest which are shown as $85,000,000. The report states that these revenues of $57,500,000 could be applied toward repayment of the reimbursable costs resulting from the allocations made to the various benefits, but it fails to state that their amount is insufficient by $26,500,000 per annum to provide for amortization (with interest) of such reimbursable costs.

Thus, by including in the tabulation of annual costs an allowance for amortization of all costs (both reimbursable and nonreimbursable) in 50 years with interest at 3 percent per annum, the impression is given at that point that provision is being made for such amortization and interest. However, in a later part of the study when the total reimbursable investment is compared with the revenues from which alone repayment of such investment could be obtained, the interest factor is disregarded.

In the other two reports, interest is likewise disregarded in the tabulations showing how the investment is to be repaid. For example, if the investment is $100,000,000, an equal annual payment for 50 years, based on interest at 3 percent compounded annually, of $3,886,-550 is required. Fifty times such annual payment is $194,327,500. The Bureau's presentation might lead the reader to believe that all that is required is $100,000,000.

In the revised report on Columbia Basin dated February 1947, it is asserted "full return of the reimbursable costs is assured" notwithstanding the uncertainties involved in estimating future revenues for some of the component projects for a period of 75 years and in estimating costs when, according to the report, "the entire plan will take many decades to accomplish."

In all three reports, one of the principal items of benefits, which are shown as greater than the annual costs, is the item "irrigation" which is stated to be the estimated increase in gross crop value which would result from irrigation. In the comments of the State of California on the Colorado River project, it is stated that such benefits should be stated on a basis of an estimated increase in net farm income not gross income. The Department of Agriculture has expressed the same viewpoint in its official comments on the Columbia River project. In all of the reports on the three basin projects, the practice is to take an assumed year's revenue and multiply it by 50 to obtain the total revenues for 50 years, whereas the annual revenues for the earlier years of a long series are generally much less.

The supplement to the Colorado River report dated July 1947, which presents the views of several States on that report, contains voluminous comments by the State of California, which, in addition to making serious reservations on the subject of engineering feasibility, makes the following specific criticisms:

1. The basis of purported showing of economic feasibility does not conform with existing law.

2. There is no justification in existing reclamation law for the consideration of economic feasibility of proposed projects on a basin-wide basis or by a comparison of estimated benefits and costs.

3. All projects previously authorized and constructed by the United States on the Colorado River system, including large developments such as the Boulder Canyon project, have been considered individually as to engineering feasibility and economic justification on a repayment basis. There appears to be no reason at this time for treating new projects on a different basis.

4. If the analysis of annual cost is based upon current prices and with more accurate cost estimates based on detailed plans, it appears that the indicated benefit-cost ratio could well be reduced to less than 1 to 1.

5. The estimate presented in the report of annual benefits is in part fallacious and in part questionable:

(a) Irrigation benefits are based on estimated increase of gross-crop income instead of increase in net farm income. (In the report of the Bureau of Reclamation on a bill to reauthorize the Gila Federal reclamation project, the irrigation benefit was estimated on the basis of net crop income.)

(b) While the report presents $65,000,000 as the annual irrigation benefit, it also shows that the water users on such projects could pay annually only $8,000,000. The use of the benefit-cost ratio as to irrigation is demonstrably fallacious.

6. The estimate of $72,000,000 for power benefits, being the estimate of gross revenue from the sale of power at an assumed rate of 4 mills per kilowatt-hour, is not supported by adequate data:

(*a*) The estimated energy output is unsubstantiated;

(*b*) The dependability of energy output and capacity is not shown;

(*c*) The ability of the market to absorb the power and the time required therefor are not shown;

(*d*) No showing is made as to whether the power could actually be sold at a price of 4 mills per kilowatt-hour;

(*e*) No analyses are presented to demonstrate that the 4-mill price would cover the actual costs of power production and transmission, including interest and amortization of capital costs of multiple-purpose works properly allocated to power and of capital costs of direct power facilities, plus the expense of operation and maintenance, replacement, and other proper charges;

(*f*) The estimated power benefits on the basis of gross power revenue appear speculative.

From the same report certain of the comments of the Department of Agriculture regarding the Colorado River report are quoted hereunder:

Some 134 potential projects or units of projects are briefly described. A substantial number of these have been investigated in detail, but for others data of only a reconnaissance nature are available.

The report recognizes that a definite economic analysis cannot be made until a final selection of projects has been made.

The over-all benefit-cost ratio presented is 1.3 to 1 at January 1940 construction costs and farm-commodity prices. Particularly in view of the phenomenal rise in construction costs since that date, and the apparent outlook for above 1940 costs for some time to come, we know you realize the precariousness of relying even upon this single over-all benefit-cost ratio as an indication of economic feasibility under present and immediately forseeable conditions.

In the revised report on the Columbia River Basin project, dated February 8, 1947, similar procedures are followed. Included in annual costs is "allowance for amortization of all construction costs in 50 years with interest at 3 percent per annum, $217,613,000," the foregoing being the amount required to amortize an investment of $5,598,484,000 (based on 1946 prices). On the same page, however, gross power revenues, some of them for periods of 75 and 77 years (on existing power projects), are stated at $8,694,695,000, and the only deduction therefrom is for operation, maintenance, and replacement costs, the remaining figure being compared with the total investment reimbursable from power revenues. By so disregarding interest, and extending the repayment period, the tabulation shows a surplus of estimated revenues over estimated reimbursable costs of $593,000,000. Actually the revenues as estimated are approximately $4,000,000,000 less than the amount required to amortize the investment in 50 years with interest at 3 percent.

In the Missouri River Basin report, similar procedures are followed. Included in annual costs is the item, "Amortization of entire cost of project at 3 percent in 50 years, $48,872,000," this being the amount required to amortize the total estimated cost of $1,257,645,700. After allocating to flood control and navigation a total of $516,545,700, the remainder of $741,100,000 is shown to be repayable. Of this amount, $318,000,000 is indicated as repayable from irrigation collections and from the sale of municipal water, and the remainder of $423,100,000 from the sale of power. The annual benefits from power of $17,141,-000 (assumed to be gross revenues), less annual operating power costs, $4,316,000, leaves $12,825,000 available annually, at full development, to repay the above indicated construction costs of $423,100,000 with interest. Since the equal annual payment required to repay this amount in 50 years with 3 percent interest compounded annually is $16,443,993, it is apparent that estimated revenues will be insufficient by $3,618,993 annually after the project reaches full development, to pay interest in full on the comparatively small part, 33.7 percent of the total construction cost to be allocated to power. On the basis of the foregoing the footnote to the tabulation of benefits, costs, and repayments, which reads as follows:

In addition to the repayments indicated, power revenues will also be sufficient to collect the interest charges on the costs allocated to power

is unwarranted. This is especially true when it is considered that if the estimated annual expenses of flood control and navigation of $4,500,000 are deducted from revenues (instead of paid from appropriations) estimated annual revenues from all sources would fall slightly short of providing for repayments of principal alone and would provide nothing whatever for interest.

AVERAGE RATE AND REPAYMENT STUDIES—BUREAU OF RECLAMATION

The Bureau of Reclamation prepares annually "Average Rate and Repayment Studies," the latest being dated January 1948. In these schedules the net operating revenues are divided into two items, first, interest on the investment allocated to power at 3 percent, and, second, the balance which is applied to principal. However, that part of the income which is described as interest is applied in the studies toward recovery of the cost of irrigation facilities (except for Boulder Canyon project and Columbia Basin project). Thus, the effect is to divide the net income into two parts, applying one to power and the other to irrigation. The column headed "Interest," computed at 3 percent on the unamortized balance of construction costs allocated to power has no significance except for the excess of such interest over irrigation costs to be repaid by power, where such an excess exists. In the narrative accompanying the schedules, interest charges are mentioned on the first page, and on the second page a statement is made that interest at the rate of 3 percent on the unamortized balance of the costs attributable to power is included in establishing average rates for firm commercial power (although under a solicitor's interpretation of the Reclamation Project Act of 1939, such rates should include 3 percent on the gross investment allocable to power). A further statement follows that interest on irrigation costs which cannot be repaid by the water users is not computed, thus giving the impression that the interest previously mentioned is real. On page 3 the narrative then states:

> The interest collected on the power allocation is credited toward defraying irrigation costs to be borne by power. That which is left after application of the interest collected is also paid by power in the repayment schedule.

At this point it seems obvious that the Bureau has come to regard interest not as an expense of the project but rather as an item of income which is collected in the rates, and that an effort had been made to make the interest item serve a dual purpose.

The same contradictory concept is expressed in a book entitled "How Reclamation Pays—1947" issued by the Bureau of Reclamation (p. IV), as follows:

> For repayment of power system costs as required by the Reclamation Project Act of 1939 and in accordance with the departmental policy of amortization of all investment allocated to power with 3 percent interest in 50 years and application of the interest component to repayment of irrigation costs that are beyond the ability of the water users to pay, see report titled "Repayment Schedules for Power Systems on Bureau of Reclamation Projects, January 1947."

It must be conceded that income which has to be applied to payment of interest cannot also be applied to the repayment of irrigation costs. Yet, in the repayment schedules referred to in the above quotation and in subsequent similar schedules this purports to be accomplished.

It is also of note in this connection that the 3-percent interest factor computed in the repayment studies is on the balance of the investment not repaid and that, in this respect, the Bureau does not follow its own solicitor's opinion. The Fowler Harper opinion, dated September 10, 1945, holds that the 3-percent interest element in the rate schedule should be calculated on the gross construction investment and not on the balance reduced by repayments.

It is realized that it will be contended that the dual treatment of the interest item is supported by legal opinion. As stated, we are not qualified to express a view as to legal matters, but as accountants we do not hesitate to comment that the practice just described impresses us as financial fantasy.

QUOTATIONS FROM CONGRESSIONAL HEARINGS

On page 32 of the hearings before the subcommittee of the Committee on Appropriations, House of Representatives, on the Interior Department appropriation bill for 1948—part 3—Bureau of Reclamation, there is given a list of investment and repayment items, which includes all projects authorized on which construction has been commenced and shows how the total amount to be expended ($1,810,000,-000) is to be repaid. The most important item is repayment by power revenues:

Power facilities (interest in addition) _____ $546, 190, 000
Irrigation cost allocated for repayment by power revenues_____ 473, 315, 000

Total _____ 1, 019, 505, 000

The words "interest in addition" may give the incorrect impression that anticipated power revenues will be sufficient to repay interest on power facilities.

In the House hearings on the Interior Department appropriation bill for 1948, pages 34 and 35, there is given a schedule of the total estimated construction costs of 73 projects to June 30, 1946, aggregating $2,086,000,000. The thirteenth column is entitled "Total" and shows $2,089,000,000, which purports (though not accurately) to be the aggregate of repayments. Against this figure there is a notation reading: "Repayments exceed construction costs." This statement is incorrect, in that columns 10, 11, and 12, which are included in the "Total," represent the following:

Authorized charge-off_____ $13, 421, 561
Flood control, navigation, and other_____ 87, 708, 999
Nonreimbursable costs authorized_____ 23, 128, 566

Total_____ 124, 259, 126

As the above items will not be recovered, it is apparent that the repayments will not equal the construction costs.

In a statement made before the House subcommittee on the Interior Department appropriation bill for 1948, Gov. Earl Warren of California said, in part, with regard to the Central Valley project:

The expenditures chargeable to hydroelectric power production must be repaid with interest. The sooner the project is completed the sooner the money will be repaid.

The Bureau of Reclamation study of this project shows total costs to be repaid from power revenues of $228,000,000, requiring, if repaid over a period of 50 years with 3 percent interest, an equal annual payment of $8,861,334, compared with annual revenues estimated at $3,506,123, and resulting in an annual deficiency of $5,355,211.

In the hearings on the Government Corporations appropriation bill for 1948, before the subcommittee of the Senate Committee on Appropriations, the following colloquy took place between Senator Homer Ferguson and Gordon R. Clapp, Chairman of the Board of Tennessee Valley Authority:

Senator FERGUSON. Do you know what the interest would have been proper on the investment? Have you paid back even enough to cover interest?
Mr. CLAPP. Well, a part of our revenues, Senator, has gone into new plant.

**104**

Senator FERGUSON. I understand that.

Mr. CLAPP. And that represents an expanded investment owned by the Government. If the net income from the TVA power operation is related to the average investment in the power facilities, it represents a return of better than 4 percent.

Senator FERGUSON. Have you paid 4 percent back into the Treasury for all money that you have had?

Mr. CLAPP. We have not paid cash back into the Treasury that would represent a payment of 4 percent.

Senator FERGUSON. Do you know how much it would amount to?

Mr. CLAPP. It could be computed.

Senator FERGUSON. Would you compute it and put it in the record for us?

Mr. CLAPP. We can do that.

The information referred to is as follows: If the payments of approximately $15,000,000 for the 2 years (which were in addition to principal and interest payments on the bonded indebtedness) were to be considered as representing interest on the appropriated funds invested in the power program, the average annual interest return for the 2 years would be 2½ percent.

## Comment on the Above

It will be noted that the information in answer to the question was not responsive, in that no figure representing interest at 4 percent on the investment was given.

The following is an extract from the testimony later in the same hearing:

Senator FERGUSON. Well, if you do not pay interest, what do you mean by the terms "self-sustaining" and "self-liquidation"? Does not the original act use those words?

Mr. CLAPP. The original act, the original and present act, use those words. That is correct.

Senator FERGUSON. If that does not mean to pay interest, what does it mean?

Mr. CLAPP. We interpret it to mean that the rates charged for the power shall be adequate to pay back the money that has been invested in the power facilities on a cash basis, in the course of providing a net income that is sufficient return on the taxpayers' money.

Senator FERGUSON. All right. You avoid that word "interest" though, is that it?

Mr. CLAPP. We avoid the word "interest," Mr. Chairman, for two reasons.

Senator FERGUSON. Well, I would like to have your reasons.

Mr. CLAPP. One is that the terms and understandings, the conditions on which this money was advanced, through appropriations instead of by bonds, carried with it no understanding with respect to a fixed payment of so many dollars per year, a certain percentage of the investment, in terms of interest. And the second reason why we do not actually make what would be called an interest payment is that the provisions of the law provide for two uses to which the surplus may be put.

One is for the conduct of the business, in maintaining and carrying on these operations and making such additions, short of dams and major plants, to the power system, so that it can carry on and fulfill its contracts with its municipal distributors and rural distributors. The other way in which those surpluses are used and the only other way in which they can be used is to go back into the Treasury as cash dividend payments.

Senator Ferguson. But if you use the terms "self-liquidating" and "self-sustaining," does not that indicate that you are to pay it back with interest? Because, after all, the Government has had a public debt during the entire period, and therefore it is to be assumed that every time they put up a dollar in this project they are paying out to some bondholder for that dollar the interest on that bond. Therefore, to make this self-sustaining and self-liquidating, it would be necessary to pay back to the taxpayers this principal, plus interest. Is that not a fair interpretation?

Mr. Clapp. That is one way to construe it, and certainly a strong argument can be made for that way of looking at it. The background and the whole history of the investment that has been made as the appropriations have gone into these projects, has been the other way—excluding a fixed interest payment.

## Comment on the Above

In view of the foregoing statements, reference is made to the statements of David E. Lilienthal, originally a director and later Chairman of TVA, in connection with the publishing of the original power rates, to the effect that it was his intention that the rates would be sufficient to pay interest on the entire debt and that the project was designed to be strictly self-supporting and self-liquidating. As our report on TVA demonstrates, net revenues are more than sufficient to amortize with interest, the costs allocated to power.

In the hearings before the subcommittee of the Committee on Appropriations, House of Representatives, on the Government corporations appropriation bill for 1948, Tennessee Valley Authority presented a justification with respect to the requirements for the 1948 program which covered 26 printed pages. In this justification, under the heading of "Power operations," the following statement was made:

Net income after all charges, including interest, is estimated to be $18,344,000 in 1948. * * *

## Comment on the Above

The reference to interest relates only to a payment of $565,000 at the rate of 1 percent on the $56,500,000 of bonds held by the United States Treasury and not to interest on the total investment of the Government. However, it is true that this was the only interest which the Authority paid in that year. Interest on the gross investment allocated to power at 3 percent per annum would have been over $13,000,000 for that year.

The phrase "after all charges" presumably includes payments in lieu of taxation which, for the fiscal year 1948, were scheduled to be 5½ percent ( 5 percent in subsequent years) of the gross proceeds from the sale of power to customers other than Government agencies and departments during the preceding year. It is of interest, in this connection, that the average rate of taxation for privately owned class A and class B electric utilities, as reported by the Federal Power Commission, was 19 percent of gross revenues.

**106**

# IV. OTHER GOVERNMENT ENTERPRISES, EXCLUSIVE OF LENDING AGENCIES

Appended hereto are our reports on the following Government enterprises, exclusive (except as to Rural Electrification Administration) of lending agencies:

United States Maritime Commission.
Rural Electrification Administration.
Panama Railroad Company.
Federal Prison Industries, Inc.
Inland Waterways Corporation and Warrior River Terminal Company.
Puerto Rico Reconstruction Administration.
The Virgin Islands Company.

Our recommendations of a general nature arising from our studies of the foregoing are presented in the introductory portion of this report; those not of general application will be found in the respective individual reports.

## United States Maritime Commission

AUGUST 17, 1948.

Hon. HERBERT HOOVER,
*Chairman, Commission on Organization of the*
*Executive Branch of the Government,*
*Washington, D. C.*

DEAR SIR: In accordance with your instructions, we have made a financial survey of United States Maritime Commission from the date of its inception, October 26, 1936, to June 30, 1947, for the purpose of assisting you in carrying out the purposes of Public Law 162, Eightieth Congress, under which your Commission was appointed.

Our survey has been based upon financial and other information available from official sources. We have regarded such information as reliable and have made no attempt to verify it through auditing procedures. Because of the fact that the subject of transportation, as a whole, which has been assigned to the Brookings Institution, includes the Maritime Commission, our survey has been confined to the financial and accounting aspects of the Commission's activities.

Moreover, we have not attempted to judge the efficiency of the management of the enterprise or the wisdom of the national policies in relation thereto as prescribed by the Congress.

We recommend:

1. That certain recommendations of the President's Advisory Committee on the Merchant Marine, referred to in 5 hereunder, be adopted.

2. That the bad accounting situation described herein be left in the hands of the groups representing the Senate Committee on Expenditures in the Executive Departments and the General Accounting Office which are at present cooperating with the Maritime Commission.

We summarize hereunder the more important facts revealed by our survey:

1. The United States Maritime Commission upon its creation by the Merchant Marine Act, 1936, succeeded to the functions, powers, and duties of the former United States Shipping Board. During the period from February 7, 1942, to September 1, 1946, the functions of the Commission were in effect divided, by Executive order of the President of the United States, into two parts, the construction of ships being the major activity of the Commission while their operation was entrusted to the War Shipping Administration.

2. From their inception until recently, the Maritime Commission and the War Shipping Administration were provided with "revolving funds" amounting in the aggregate to more than $20,000,000,000. As shown more fully later in this report the combined net worth at June 30, 1945 (the latest date for which reliable information is available, was somewhat under $15,000,000,000. Since that date many vessels, both large and small, have been sold and payments of large amounts have been made to the Treasury of the United States. In consequence it may be presumed that net worth at this time is much less than at June 30, 1945.

3. The accounts of the Maritime Commission (and of the dissolved War Shipping Administration) are very much in arrears and reliable information as to financial condition is presently unobtainable from them for any recent date.

4. At the present time a survey of the Commission is being made by representatives of the Senate Committee on Expenditures in the Executive Departments and several groups representing the General Accounting Office are assisting the Commission in its efforts to surmount the accounting difficulties mentioned above.

5. There have been extensive hearings before various committees of the Congress with respect to the Maritime Commission and the War Shipping Administration and various special reports dealing with them have been issued. Among these is that of the President's Advi-

sory Committee on the Merchant Marine which was headed by K. T. Keller, president of Chrysler Corp., and included a number of the Nation's business leaders. The report of this committee, dated November 1947, contains, among others, the following recommendations:

a. That executive and operative functions now assigned to the Commission to be vested in a single administrator who in time of peace would report to the Secretary of Commerce.

b. That a Maritime Board composed of the five commissioners exercise the quasi-legislative and quasi-judicial functions for which the Commission is presently responsible.

c. That a revolving fund of limited amount be restored, or a separate shipbuilding authorization with suitable contract authority be established, preferably the former.

Our more detailed comments follow:

CREATION AND AUTHORITY

The United States Maritime Commission was created by the Merchant Marine Act, 1936 (49 Stat. 1985) to further the development and maintenance of an adequate and well-balanced American merchant marine, to promote the commerce of the United States, and to aid in the national defense. Under the act creating it there were vested in the Commission the functions, powers, and duties of the former United States Shipping Board under the preceding acts of 1916, 1920, 1922, and 1928. While the act creating the Commission received the President's signature on June 29, 1936, it was not until October 26, 1936, that the Commission became fully clothed with its administrative powers.

By Executive Order 9054, dated February 7, 1942, issued under the First War Powers Act, the War Shipping Administration was established within the Office for Emergency Management of the Executive Office of the President. By this order there were transferred to the Administrator of the War Shipping Administration, among other things, the functions, duties, and powers, with respect to the operation, purchase, charter, insurance, repair, maintenance, and requisition of vessels and requisite facilities, which had been vested in the United States Maritime Commission by the Merchant Marine Act, 1936, as amended. In effect, this Executive order split the former activities of the Maritime Commission into two divisions: The major activity of the Commission became the construction of ships while their operation was entrusted to the War Shipping Administration.

On September 1, 1946, pursuant to the provisions of section 202 of the act of July 8, 1946 (60 Stat. 501), all functions of the War Shipping Administration were transferred back to the United States Maritime Commission for the purpose of liquidation of the former by December 31, 1946. Thereafter, the authority of the Maritime Commission to perform the functions transferred from the War Shipping Administration was successively extended by acts of Congress.

Administration of the Maritime Commission is vested in a commission of five members appointed by the President with the advice and consent of the Senate, with not more than three members being of the same political party. The Administrator of the War Shipping Administration was appointed, under Executive Order 9054, by the President. During the entire life of the War Shipping Administration its Administrator was a member of the Maritime Commission who, except for a period of a few months, was also Chairman of the Commission.

### ACTIVITIES

With respect to the ship-construction function there follows a summary accounting for large vessels (over 1,500 dead-weight tons) from inception of the United States Maritime Commission to June 30, 1947, based upon a report of the General Accounting Office:

| | Total vessels | War constructed vessels | Prewar vessels |
|---|---|---|---|
| Vessels owned, June 29, 1936 | 149 | _____ | 149 |
| Acquired to June 30, 1947: | | | |
| Constructed by U. S. Maritime Commission | 4, 558 | 4, 558 | _____ |
| By purchase, etc | 630 | 89 | 541 |
| From other Government agencies | 302 | 124 | 178 |
| Total acquired | 5, 490 | 4, 771 | 719 |
| Total to be accounted for | 5, 639 | 4, 771 | 868 |
| Deductions to June 30, 1947: | | | |
| Sold under Merchant Ship Sales Act of 1946 | 1, 105 | 1, 105 | _____ |
| Sold under Merchant Marine Act: | | | |
| For scrapping | 170 | 15 | 155. |
| For operation | 165 | 13 | 152 |
| Transferred to other Government agencies | 200 | 182 | 18 |
| Vessels lost | 427 | 294 | 133 |
| Returned to former owners | 52 | 2 | 50 |
| Vessels abandoned | 2 | 1 | 1 |
| Total deductions | 2, 121 | 1, 612 | 509 |
| Vessels owned, June 30, 1947 | 3, 518 | 3, 159 | 359 |

Since June 30, 1947, sales of vessels to June 30, 1948, have been reported as follows:

Under Merchant Ship Sales Act of 1946_____ 606
Other (approximately—including "landing ship tanks" received during the year from other Government departments)_____ 735

In addition, purchase applications under the Merchant Ship Sales Act of 1946 have been approved for 79 vessels as to which title had not yet been passed at June 30, 1948.

**110**

The quarterly report to Congress required by the Merchant Ship Sales Act of 1946 (relating to war constructed vessels), for the quarter ended June 30, 1948, states the number of vessels available for sale at 2,267. This is 207 less than the number (2,474) arrived at by deducting sales and approved purchase applications from the vessels owned at June 30, 1947. We are informed that a part of this difference is represented by tankers and other vessels transferred to the Navy, or other Government departments, but that this does not account fully for the discrepancy and that the "available" figure of 2,267 is subject to a degree of error.

The sales shown above of approximately 735 vessels other than under the Merchant Ship Sales Act of 1946 include more than 450 LSTs. The exact number of vessels owned at June 30, 1948, held for sale other than under the Merchant Ship Sales Act of 1946 is not known at this writing but a report of the Bureau of the Reserve Fleet as of that date indicates that 76 over-age vessels were then in the reserve fleet.

The cost of the vessels owned at June 30, 1948, is not presently available from the records but an approximate valuation based upon the "floor" sales prices published in the Federal Register in accordance with General Order No. 60 has been given us by the Division of Large Vessel Sales. This valuation, for the 2,267 vessels referred to, is $1,474,769,034, representing an average of approximately $650,500 a vessel. The Division informs us that it is unable to estimate the value of the 76 over-age vessels.

The aggregate of vessel sales to June 30, 1948, is shown by reports of the Maritime Commission to have been as follows:

|  | Vessels | Approximate proceeds |
|---|---|---|
| Under Merchant Ship Sales Act of 1946 | [1] 1, 790 | [1] $1, 720, 000, 000 |
| Other than under that act | 1, 033 | 49, 128, 361 |

[1] Includes 79 vessels as to which title has not passed.

All of the foregoing relates to vessels of more than 1,500 deadweight tons. With respect to smaller vessels, it is reported by the Small Vessels Division of the Maritime Commission that during the year ended June 30, 1948, 2,737 small vessels were disposed of for $22,483,396 and that at June 30, 1948, there were 92 vessels having a declared value of $22,689,733 remaining to be disposed of.

It is of interest that the Small Vessels Division disposes not only of the small vessels of the Maritime Commission but also of small vessels of various types for other Government agencies, principally the Army, Navy, and Coast Guard.

As to the operating functions (of the War Shipping Administration) it is stated that at the end of the war with Japan that Administration controlled 4,221 vessels aggregating 44,940,000 dead-weight tonnage.

## Financial Aspects

Because of the condition of the accounts of the United States Maritime Commission and the War Shipping Administration (to which further reference will be made) it is impracticable to present a summary of the financial results of operations for recent periods. However, the following summarizes their financial condition (in millions of dollars) in the aggregate at June 30, 1945, the latest date for which audited (though not fully approved) figures are available:

|  | *Millions* |
|---|---|
| Net appropriations and allotments, including assets of former U. S. Shipping Board, and miscellaneous items | $21,794.4 |

| Less: | |
|---|---|
| Deficits to June 30, 1945: | |
| U. S. Maritime Commission | 503.9 |
| War Shipping Administration | 3,668.7 |
| Expenditures and unliquidated obligations, less recoverable items and property (War Shipping Administration—Defense aid program and UNRRA program) | 2,797.1 |
| Total deductions | 6,969.7 |

| Remainder—net worth, June 30, 1945: | |
|---|---|
| U. S. Maritime Commission | 5,022.4 |
| War Shipping Administration | 9,802.3 |
| Total | 14,824.7 |

The combined net worth of $14,824,700,000 shown above was represented by the following:

### Assets

|  | *Millions* |
|---|---|
| General funds with Treasurer of United States and cash in custody of vessel operating agents, etc | $ 5,346.4 |
| Notes and receivables | 480.5 |
| Inventories | 87.7 |
| Vessels and floating equipment | 10,365.2 |
| Other property | 561.3 |
| Other assets (includes capital stock of American Presidents Lines, $2.7) | 272.2 |
| Total assets | 17,113.3 |

### Liabilities

|  |  |
|---|---|
| Accounts payable—contractors, vendors, and others | 1,687.2 |
| Working funds—Government departments | 286.5 |
| Other liabilities and credits | 314.9 |
| Total liabilities | 2,288.6 |
| Remainder—net worth | 14,824.7 |

**112**

It will be observed from the above that at June 30, 1945, the Maritime Commission was carrying as an asset certain capital stock of American Presidents Lines, Ltd. This stock is stated to represent approximately 93 percent of the voting power and approximately 79 percent of the common-stock equity of the corporation and is carried on the books at a valuation of $2,666,030. On the basis of financial statements for the year ended December 31, 1947, forming part of the annual report to stockholders for that year, it appears that the consolidated net worth of the company and its subsidiary at December 31, 1947, was in excess of $22,000,000. The Commission acquired the stock in 1938 in connection with the reorganization of Dollar Steamship Lines, Inc., Ltd. We understand that the Commission's title to the stock is being questioned at law and that plans to dispose of it are consequently in abeyance at this time.

In connection with the data just presented, and the accounting difficulties referred to, it should be pointed out that under the "Legislative Reorganization Act of 1946," approved August 2, 1946, provision is made, among other things, for the creation at the commencement of each Congress, of various standing committees of the Senate and House of Representatives, among these being, in each body, a Committee on Expenditures in the Executive Department. It is provided in the act that "all proposed legislation, messages, petitions, memorials, and other matters" relating to "budget and accounting measures, other than appropriations" and to "reorganizations in the Executive Branch of the Government" shall be referred to these committees (subject to certain exceptions in the case of the House of Representatives).

The committee (of the Senate) has the duty of:

a. Receiving and examining reports of the Comptroller General of the United States and of submitting such recommendations to the Senate as it deems necessary or desirable in connection with the subject matter of such reports;

b. Studying the operation of Government activities at all levels with a view to determining its economy and efficiency;

c. Evaluating the effects of laws enacted to reorganize the legislative and executive branches of the Government;

d. Studying intergovernmental relationships between the United States and the States and municipalities, and between the United States and international organizations of which the United States is a member.

The Senate committee, consisting of 13 members under the chairmanship of Senator George D. Aiken, through a group headed by Mr. E. B. Van Horn, staff director of the committee, is presently making what is described as a "management survey" of the Maritime Commission. It appears that a corresponding committee of the House of Representatives is not functioning so far as the Maritime Commission is concerned for the reason that, under one of the rules of the act, the subject remains within the jurisdiction of the House Committee on Merchant Marine and Fisheries. The latter committee is not, we are informed, currently active in pursuing the matters referred to in the hearings mentioned on page 117 hereof and has not brought in recent reports thereon.

## ACCOUNTING

The accounts of the United States Maritime Commission are presently, and for several years have been, in a deplorable condition. This fact has been known to the Congress for the past 2 years, the proceedings of several of its committees containing considerable testimony on the subject. In spite, however, of efforts which have been made by the Maritime Commission to bring its accounts up to date there remains a tremendous "backlog" of work to be performed. This backlog includes especially the processing of claims both in favor of and against the Government (with respect, among other things, to vessel inventories and to voyage accounts) as to which the Maritime Commission estimates a net recovery of somewhere in the neighborhood of $50,000,000 may be effected.

This portion of the backlog should be distinguished from that considerable portion in which the possibility of direct financial savings or recoveries does not exist. It is, of course, not open to dispute that delays in the processing of claims necessarily reduce the chance of recovery thereon.

At the present time, as has already been stated, the Senate Committee on Expenditures in the Executive Departments is engaged in making a management survey of the Maritime Commission under the very broad powers of that committee as prescribed in the "Legislative Reorganization Act of 1946." The Committee on Merchant Marine and Fisheries of the House of Representatives has also been giving attention to the Commission's accounts during the past 2 years. Under these conditions it has seemed neither necessary nor desirable for us to make a detailed study of the condition of the accounts or the methods followed in keeping them.

That the condition of the accounts is truly deplorable is evidenced by the following:

1. No formal balance sheet of the Commission or statement of its income and expenses has been prepared since those of June 30, 1945.

2. The latest quarterly balance sheet and statement of income and expense filed with the Treasury Department as required by Executive orders was as of March 31, 1947 (February 28, 1947, as to certain functions of War Shipping Administration), and these statements are known to be extremely inaccurate as will be shown later in this report. Filing of subsequent reports, as required quarterly, has not, we are informed, been attempted because of the condition of the accounts.

3. At the present time the accounts have not been completely posted and adjusted for the fiscal years 1946 and 1947 which is a prerequisite to the preparation of adequate financial statements.

114

4. The present "backlog" of accounting work in arrears is estimated by the staff of the Maritime Commission to represent approximately 2,200 man-years of work.

5. As the inevitable result of items 3 and 4, the accounts for the current fiscal year do not as yet reflect assets and liabilities of several billions of dollars.

The points set forth above will be discussed in greater detail in the following paragraphs:

*Item 1*

It has already been stated herein that no formal balance sheet and income statement are available for any date subsequent to June 30, 1945. The statements as of that date were audited by the Audit Division of the General Accounting Office whose reports thereon (dated April 17, 1947, as to the Maritime Commission and April 30, 1947, as to War Shipping Administration) were transmitted to the Congress. These reports reiterate the same general objections to the accounting methods and procedures employed as had been voiced in the reports on the audits for the fiscal years 1943 and 1944. Moreover, both of the reports for the fiscal year 1945 state in conclusion as follows (except for the difference in names):

The accompanying financial statements reflect the administrative balance sheet as of June 30, 1945, and the operating statement for the fiscal year then ended, as adjusted by the major corrections resulting from the audit; but due to the conditions set forth in this report, it is not possible to state that such financial statements present fairly the position of the United States Maritime Commission at June 30, 1945, and the results of its operations for the fiscal year, in conformity with generally accepted accounting principles.

It is apparent from the foregoing that the financial statements as of June 30, 1945, even as revised extensively under the audit of the General Accounting Office, still failed to meet with the complete approval of the General Accounting Office.

*Item 2*

The audit report of the General Accounting Office for the fiscal years ended June 30, 1946 and 1947, is dated March 26, 1948. This report states, among other things, "The accounting records for the fiscal years 1946 and 1947 have not been completely recorded or adjusted to the facts. On the whole, the accounting records were in even worse condition than in the prior years."

In spite of the stated condition of the records the quarterly statements required under Budget-Treasury Regulation 3 were submitted to the Treasury Department for the quarters ended September 1945, March, June, September, and December, 1946, and March 1947, although to an important extent at least some of them represented information not of record in the books of account. We were informed that this was done under an understanding with the Treasury Department with respect to the approximate nature of the statements.

To show the unreliability of the figures so furnished to the Treasury Department (and published by it) the following comparison is made between total assets (expressed in millions of dollars) of United States Maritime Commission and War Shipping Administration as stated in annual reports of the Secretary of the Treasury and in audit reports of the General Accounting Office:

|  | U.S.M.C. | W.S.A. | Combined |
|---|---|---|---|
| At June 30, 1944: | | | |
| Per Secretary of Treasury [1] | $9, 132 | $1, 086 | $10, 218 |
| Per audit reports [2] | 5, 212 | 9, 087 | 14, 299 |
| Difference | [3] 3, 920 | 8, 001 | 4, 081 |
| At June 30, 1945: | | | |
| Per Secretary of Treasury [4] | 4, 073 | 7, 854 | 11, 927 |
| Per audit reports [5] | 6, 537 | 10, 576 | 17, 113 |
| Difference | 2, 464 | 2, 722 | 5, 186 |

[1] Report dated Jan. 3, 1945.
[2] Reports dated June 25, 1946.
[3] Red.
[4] Report dated Jan. 21, 1946.
[5] Reports dated Apr. 17 and 30, 1947.

Similar comparisons to the above cannot be made as of June 30, 1946 and 1947, for the reason that the General Accounting Office deemed it impracticable, as set forth in the audit report for years ended those dates, to prepare financial statements and that the Commission itself made no such statement subsequent to March 31, 1947.

It is apparent from the foregoing that the figures submitted by the Maritime Commission and the War Shipping Administration to the Treasury Department for the fiscal years 1944 and 1945, and used in the annual report of the Treasurer of the United States, were very inaccurate. Moreover, the audit report for the fiscal years 1946 and 1947 states that the transactions of those years had not been completely recorded. It therefore follows that the amounts shown in the reports of the Secretary of the Treasury for the fiscal years 1946 and 1947 with respect to the Maritime Commission and War Shipping Administration, having been supplied by those organizations on the basis of admittedly incomplete records, supplemented by special tabulations and computations, must be regarded as subject to a practical certainty of very material errors. Nevertheless, there is no indication in the report of the Secretary of the Treasury for the year ended June 30, 1947, that this is so, and there is wholly inadequate indication of a formal character in the statements furnished to the Treasury Department that they should be regarded as lacking in reliability.

In this connection it should also be noted that in the Daily Statement of the United States Treasury as of June 15, 1948, the same stale and inaccurate figures of March 31 and February 28, 1947, are still carried, with no more indication of their unreliability than is implied by the mere statement of their date.

### Items 3, 4, and 5

It has been stated herein that as the inevitable result of items 3 and 4 (pp. 114 and 115), the accounts of the Commission do not as yet reflect the assets and liabilities of the Commission.   It is a fact that a trial balance of the general ledger as of March 31, 1948, was achieved about the middle of May 1948, but such trial balance does not include important amounts which must be brought forward from 1946 and 1947 accounts when such amounts are eventually established.   For example, the cost (or other) value of vessels owned at July 1, 1947, has not been recorded in the general books for the current fiscal year, and this is also true of other assets and liabilities.   Under these conditions, the accomplishment of a trial balance of the 1948 ledger means no more than that the posting of current transactions appears to have been made with clerical accuracy and is nearly up to date; proper adjustment of the 1946 and 1947 accounts remains a prerequisite to the preparation of adequate financial statements as of current dates.

In its efforts to cope with the "backlog" which still exists, the Commission's staff has made what appears to be a careful survey and has prepared plans for carrying out the work, including formal instructions for the guidance of the staff to be assigned.   These plans were based upon the employment of additional personnel for which Congress has refused to appropriate; the opinion has been advanced, however, that by revision of certain auditing and other procedures it may be possible to make personnel available for the backlog work. Unless radical reductions in routine are made, it appears that the personnel requested by the Commission in the 1949 budget "justifications" (480 persons at a cost of $1,556,069) would require several years to complete the work of eliminating the backlog.

Following is further information bearing on the accounting difficulties of the Maritime Commission and the War Shipping Administration:

The annual report of the Maritime Commission to Congress for the year ended June 30, 1942, contained a balance sheet and a statement of income and expenses; none of the subsequent reports has contained these important statements.

The reports of the General Accounting Office and the audit of the accounts of the Maritime Commission and the War Shipping Administration for the years ended June 30, 1943 (not dated) and 1944 (dated June 25, 1946) contained many and severe criticisms of the accounts of those agencies of the Government.   These reports were the subject of hearings before the Committee on the Merchant Marine and Fisheries of the House of Representatives (79th Cong., 2d sess.) during July 1946.

**117**

The hearings were concerned principally with consideration of these criticisms, the responses of the Maritime Commission and the War Shipping Administration thereto, and related testimony. It may be noted at this point that it was testified before that committee that an audit in 1943 by the General Accounting Office of the balance sheet of the Maritime Commission (presumably of June 30, 1942) was not completed because the details of numerous adjustments made in the balance sheet could not be obtained. Subsequently (January 3, 1947), the committee brought in a report (Union Calendar No. 1) concurring generally in the criticisms made by the Comptroller General and making various recommendations for correction of the existing situation. This report included a report of Col. Sivert M. Wedeberg and Lt. Comdr. C. Wilbur Cissell, accounting advisers to the committee, which also concurred generally in the criticisms of the Comptroller General. Another report was also made on the activities of the committee during 1946 (Union Calendar No. 4, January 3, 1947).

As a result of the proceedings just described, and at the suggestion of the House committee, a joint committee of six members was formed in November 1946 consisting of three representatives of the Maritime Commission and three of the General Accounting Office to study and make recommendations concerning (1) improvement, simplification, and coordination in the existing accounting system; (2) proper objectives of accounting; and (3) the designing and installation of an accounting system suited to the needs of both agencies. The work performed by this accounting committee is summarized in a report which, with various other communications from the committee, was transmitted to counsel for the House committee by letter of Admiral William Ward Smith, Chairman, United States Maritime Commission, dated June 13, 1947. As of September 3, 1947, due to organizational changes, including the appointment as Chief of the Bureau of Accounts of the member of the General Accounting Office who had theretofore served as chairman of the joint committee, this committee was disbanded.

The fact that its accounts were not in good order was acknowledged officially by the Maritime Commission in its annual report to the Congress for the fiscal year ended June 30, 1947, which was transmitted to Congress by letter of the Chairman, Admiral Smith, under date of December 4, 1947. This report contains the following (pp. 34 and 35) under the subtitle "Accounting":

During the fiscal year 1947 the accounting system and procedures of the Maritime Commission were criticized by the General Accounting Office, several congressional committees, and the Bureau of the Budget. During the war it was impossible to get personnel to keep pace with the greatly increased accounting responsibilities of the Commission and the War Shipping Administration.

In order to protect the Government's interests and to insure that it was not penalized under the cost-plus and price-minus types of contracts, the Commission concentrated the work of its accounting personnel on field auditing. This built up a backlog of posting and analysis too great to be handled by the insufficient personnel available in the Washington office, and it was impossible to produce required statements of profit and loss and balance sheets within a reasonable time after the closing of an accounting period.

In November 1946, a joint accounting committee composed of three representatives from the Commission and three from the General Accounting Office was appointed to look into the various problems of the Commission's accounting. It was given authority to develop an accounting system which would be acceptable to the Comptroller General of the United States and serve to develop the information required by the various congressional committees and the Bureau of the Budget. This committee developed a chart of control accounts and established an "allotment ledger control system" in the Maritime Commission. Allowing for the education of personnel in maintenance of these charts, the required information for presentation of budget estimates will be available for the fiscal year 1949. Copies of all recommendations submitted by this committee have been forwarded to the Comptroller General.

On April 7, 1947, the Joint Accounting Committee recommended that the Maritime Commission and the Comptroller General jointly request sufficient personnel to bring all of the accounts of the Commission up to date. It was anticipated that employees required, on a temporary basis not to exceed 1 year, would be 189, at a cost of some $796,000, in addition to personnel requested in the estimates then pending before the Congress. It was further anticipated that the expenditure of this estimated $796,000 would result in the reclamation of some $70,000,-000 owing to the Government by virtue of accounts receivable and claims of the Government not yet processed.

Since this sum was not included in the Commission's appropriations, the backlogs which existed at the time of this recommendation still exist within the Commission. All available personnel at this time is required to maintain the current work load of the Commission.

The condition referred to appears to have deteriorated still further, as is asserted by the report of the General Accounting Office dated March 26, 1948, on its audit for the fiscal years ended June 30, 1946 and 1947, from which a quotation has already been made on page 115 hereof. This report concludes with the following:

In view of the incomplete and inaccurate condition of the accounting records, it was not practicable to prepare financial statements for the Maritime Commission and War Shipping Administration showing the results of operation for the fiscal years 1946 and 1947 and the financial position at the close of the respective fiscal periods, and, therefore, it is not possible to furnish a certificate in this connection in accordance with generally accepted accounting practice.

During the course of the audit covered by this report, the various deficiencies and shortcomings which were found were discussed with the officials within the Maritime Commission in charge of the functions involved. Invariably, these officials readily admitted the unreasonableness of the delays, the inadequacy of the accounts, and the like. Uniformly, however, their contention was that these conditions stemmed from a lack of sufficient personnel to do the work properly, the necessary result of insufficient appropriations by the Congress. Such contention is referred to in this report solely as representing the position of the Maritime Commission on these matters. The audit did not disclose information sufficient to permit an expression of opinion as to the merits of the contention.

In explanation of recent efforts of the Maritime Commission to improve its accounting situation, letters of March 12 and May 27, 1948, were addressed to Hon. Richard B. Wigglesworth, Appropriations Subcommittee, House of Representatives, and Hon. George D. Aiken, chairman, Committee on Expenditures in the Executive Departments, United States Senate, respectively, by Admiral William Ward Smith, chairman of United States Maritime Commission, and testimony was given by Admiral Smith, Commissioner Joseph K. Carson, Jr., and others before subcommittees of Appropriation Committees of the Senate and the House of Representatives during April, May, and June, 1948.

It will be apparent from the matters referred to in this report that there is considerable knowledge on the part of the Congress of the condition of the accounts of the Maritime Commission, and that steps toward corrective measures are being taken. We understand that the report on the Maritime Commission of the staff director of the Senate Committee on Expenditures in the Executive Departments will be rendered to that committee about November 1948, and that in the meantime various recommendations by the representatives of the committee have been put into effect.

Yours truly,

HASKINS & SELLS.

## Rural Electrification Administration

AUGUST 23, 1948.

HON. HERBERT HOOVER,
    *Chairman, Commission on Organization of the*
        *Executive Branch of the Government,*
            *Washington, D. C.*

DEAR SIR: In accordance with your instructions, we have made a financial survey of Rural Electrification Administration (REA) from the date of its inception, May 11, 1935, to March 31, 1948, for the purpose of assisting you in carrying out the purposes of Public Law 162, Eightieth Congress, under which your Commission was appointed.

Our survey has been based upon financial and other information available from official sources. We have regarded such information as reliable and have made no attempt to verify it through auditing procedures.

Moreover, we have not attempted to judge the efficiency of the management of the enterprise or the wisdom of the national policies in relation thereto as prescribed by the Congress.

We summarize hereunder the more important facts revealed by our survey.

1. References have repeatedly been made in the annual reports of the Administrator of the Rural Electrification Administration to the Secretary of Agriculture to the opposition of public utility companies, including assertions that in some cases "spite lines" have been estab-

120

lished by them. On the other hand, testimony by officials of a number of utility companies before the Subcommittee of the House Committee on Appropriations at hearings on the Department of Agriculture appropriation bill for 1948 (we have not examined the records of other hearings) cites a number of cases in which it is asserted that REA has caused the duplication of existing facilities in contravention of the intent of the law. We do not express an opinion as to the merits of any of these contentions.

2. From the inception of REA to March 31, 1948, loans aggregating $1,259,935,461 were allocated to 1,034 borrowers to whom actual advances of $877,716,224 were made. The amount of loans outstanding at March 31, 1948, was $786,223,099. The aggregate amount of installments of principal and interest overdue more than 30 days was $1,077,165 while, on the other hand, advance payments by borrowers were $19,239,821. Further analysis of these figures is given on page 125 of this report.

3. At March 31, 1948, REA had a deficit of $11,369,093 representing the accumulated excess of expenses, principally interest on borrowings (but not on direct appropriations) and administrative expenses, over interest income. The administrative expenses have been met by special appropriations, the total thereof to June 30, 1947, having been approximately $36,000,000 and that for 1948 being $5,000,000. If the functions of REA were confined to the granting and collection of loans the administration expenses would be considered unreasonably high in relation to the loans handled, but they include other activities not directly related to lending, such as construction assistance to cooperatives, and legal, engineering, and accounting advice to borrowers. On the other hand, administrative expenses are not charged with some services or expenses incidental to REA activities, as, for example, legal services rendered by the office of the Solicitor of the Department of Agriculture, and rental expense covered by appropriations to Public Buildings Administration.

4. REA has received direct appropriations of $145,000,000 for loans and purchases of property on which it pays no interest. On funds borrowed by it (from Reconstruction Finance Corporation prior to July 1, 1947, and thereafter from the United States Treasury) the rate of interest was 3 percent per annum to September 21, 1944, and 1.75 percent since that date. The rate charged by REA to its borrowers, on the other hand, averaged approximately 2.6 percent to September 21, 1944, and was reduced to a flat 2 percent on that date. Thus, up to September 21, 1944, an interest loss of 0.4 percent was sustained on all funds borrowed and loaned, while since that date an interest profit of 0.25 percent has been realized.

5. Since July 1, 1947, the date the Treasury was prescribed by the Congress as the source of loans to REA, all collections by REA,

whether of principal or interest, are required to be paid to the Treasury and applied in part to payment of interest on loans from the Treasury and the remainder in reduction of such loans. After all loans have been repaid, all collections of principal and interest are to be covered into the Treasury as miscellaneous receipts. It should be noted that all collections of principal and interest on loans made from appropriations (which are non-interest-bearing) are treated by the Treasury as repayments of interest-bearing debt or as interest thereon.

6. No amount is included as a charge against revenues for Federal, State, and local taxes which would be payable if the REA program were operated by private interests instead of by cooperatives financed by the Federal Government.

7. The retail electric operating revenue of the borrowers from REA for the 9 months ended March 31, 1948, was $90,315,275. Since most of these borrowers are cooperatives, the Federal Government is deprived of the 3⅓-percent electric-energy tax which would be paid by the consumers if the energy represented were furnished by private corporations.

8. No commercial type audit of the accounts of REA has been made by the General Accounting Office and no audit report thereon is available. We have been informed by the General Accounting Office that its files pertaining to other audits of REA accounts show no record of criticisms, any exceptions taken by its representatives having been adjusted in an informal manner.

Our more detailed comments follow:

AUTHORIZATION

The Rural Electrification Administration was created by Executive Order 7037, of May 11, 1935, under authority of the Emergency Relief Appropriation Act of 1935, approved April 8, 1935 (49 Stat. 115), "to initiate, formulate, administer, and supervise a program of approved projects with respect to the generation, transmission, and distribution of electric energy in rural areas." The functions of the agency were defined more specifically by Executive Order 7130, dated August 7, 1935.

Statutory provision for the agency was made in the Rural Electrification Act of 1936, approved May 20, 1936 (49 Stat. 1363, 7 U. S. Code, ch. 31). REA became a part of the Department of Agriculture under Reorganization Plan II, effective July 1, 1939. Title IV of the Work Relief and Public Works Appropriation Act of 1938, approved June 21, 1938 ("Rural Electrification Act of 1938," 52 Stat. 818) authorized further borrowing from the Reconstruction Finance Corporation and added a requirement that borrowers from REA agree to use materials and supplies produced in the United States. Title V of the Department of Agriculture Organic Act of 1944 approved September 21, 1944, liberalized the terms of REA loans and removed the time limitation from its lending program. On December 23, 1944, The Rural Electrification Act was further amended to authorize REA to refinance certain rural electrification obligations owed to the Tennessee Valley Authority (58 Stat. 925). The Department of Agriculture Appropriation Act, 1948, approved July 30, 1947 (61 Stat. 546) further amended the Rural Electrification Act by transferring from the Reconstruction Finance Corporation to the Secretary of the Treasury the authority to make loans to REA.

FINANCING

Section 3 (a) of the Rural Electrification Act of 1936 as amended by the Department of Agriculture Appropriation Act 1948, approved July 30, 1947 (61 Stat. 546) authorizes the Secretary of the Treasury "to make loans to the Administrator, * * * in such amounts in the aggregate for each fiscal year commencing with the fiscal year ending June 30, 1948, as the Congress may from time to time determine to be necessary, either without interest or at such rate of interest per annum, not in excess of the rate provided for in sections 4 and 5 (the rate of interest charged borrowers by REA of 2 percent) of this act, as the Secretary of the Treasury may determine, upon the security of the obligations of borrowers from the Administrator * * *. Interest rates on the unpaid balace of any loans made by Reconstruction Finance Corporation to the Administrator prior to July 1, 1947, shall be adjusted to the interest rate, if any, established for loans made after June 30, 1947, in accordance with the foregoing provision * * *." A contract between the Acting Secretary of the Treasury and the Administrator dated August 8, 1947, fixed the rate to be charged to REA from July 1, 1947, at the average rate at the beginning of each fiscal year on the outstanding interest-bearing marketable Public Debt obligations of the United States; but not in excess of 2 percent and where such average rate is not a multiple of one-eighth of 1 percent, the rate to be the multiple of one-eighth of 1 percent next lower than such average rate.

From the inception of REA on May 11, 1935, until June 30, 1936, funds for rural electrification loans and for administrative expenses were allotted by the President from funds made available by the Emergency Relief Appropriation Act of 1935. Since June 30, 1936, the administrative expenses have been provided for by direct appropriations. Funds for rural electrification loans were provided from June 30, 1936, to June 30, 1947, by borrowing from Reconstruction Finance Corporation, or by direct appropriations. As previously stated, the interest rate on borrowings from Reconstruction Finance Corporation was reduced from 3 percent to 1.75 percent, effective September 21, 1944.

REA borrowings from Reconstruction Finance Corporation and the Treasury authorized from the inception of REA to June 30, 1948, together with a summary of appropriations during that period follows:

| Fiscal year | Borrowings authorized for loans and purchases of property | Appropriations | |
|---|---|---|---|
| | | For loans and purchases of property | For administrative expenses |
| May 11, 1945 to June 30, 1936_____ | _____ | $15, 000, 000 | $743, 408 |
| 1937 [1]_____ | $50, 000, 000 | _____ | 1, 201, 617 |
| 1938_____ | _____ | 30, 000, 000 | 1, 520, 000 |
| 1939 [1]_____ | 100, 000, 000 | 40, 000, 000 | 2, 402, 000 |
| 1940_____ | _____ | 40, 000, 000 | 2, 790, 000 |
| 1941 [1]_____ | 100, 000, 000 | _____ | 3, 673, 425 |
| 1942 [1]_____ | 100, 000, 000 | _____ | 4, 262, 375 |
| 1943 [1]_____ | 10, 000, 000 | _____ | 3, 500, 000 |
| 1944_____ | _____ | 20, 000, 000 | 2, 558, 000 |
| 1945 [1]_____ | 25, 000, 000 | _____ | 3, 246, 000 |
| 1946 [1]_____ | 300, 000, 000 | _____ | 4, 181, 965 |
| 1947 [1]_____ | 250, 000, 000 | _____ | 5, 550, 000 |
| 1948 [2]_____ | 225, 000, 000 | _____ | 5, 000, 000 |
| Total_____ | 1, 160, 000, 000 | 145, 000, 000 | 40, 628, 790 |

[1] From Reconstruction Finance Corporation.
[2] From United States Treasury.

## LOANS TO REA BORROWERS

Section 4 of the Rural Electrification Act of 1936 provided that the Administrator is empowered to make loans to persons, private corporations, and public bodies "for the purpose of financing the construction and operation of generating plants, electric transmission and distribution lines or systems for the furnishing of electric energy to persons in rural areas who are not receiving central station service"; specified that preference in making loans be given to cooperative associations and public bodies; and specified "that all such loans shall be self-liquidating within a period of not to exceed 25 years and shall bear interest at a rate equal to the average rate of interest payable by the United States on its obligations, having a maturity of 10 or more years after the dates thereof, issued during the last preceding fiscal year in which any such obligations were issued." The interest rates at which loans were made under this provision were as follows:

Fiscal year—                                                         *Percent*
   1937_____ 2. 77
   1938_____ 2. 88
   1939_____ 2. 73
   1940_____ 2. 69
   1941_____ 2. 46
   1942_____ 2. 48
   1943_____ 2. 57
  July, 1, 1943 to Sept. 21, 1944_____ 2. 49

124

Section 5 of the act authorized, for the purpose of financing the wiring of farmsteads and the acquisition of electrical and plumbing equipment, loans to the borrowers of funds under section 4 or to any person, firm or corporation supplying or installing wiring, appliances or equipment, at the same rate of interest as is referred to above under section 4. Section 3 (a) of the act limited the repayment of these types of loans to not more than two-thirds of the "assured life" of the wiring and equipment and not more than 5 years.

The interest rate of loans made under the Emergency Relief Appropriation Act of 1935 was 3 percent.

Title V of the Department of Agriculture Organic Act of 1944, approved September 21, 1944, reduced the rates on the unmatured and unpaid balances of the loans made prior to the effective date of that act to a flat 2 percent and provided that loans made thereafter be made at 2 percent. This act also increased the permissible maximum amortization period on loans for generation, transmission, and distribution facilities from 25 to 35 years.

The status of REA lending activities at March 31, 1948 as indicated by its balance sheet and by its statistical summary as of that date, is summarized below:

Loans outstanding to REA borrowers_____$786, 223, 099
Loan allocations (cumulative, rescissions deducted) :

| | Number of borrowers | Amount |
|---|---|---|
| Cooperatives_____ | 952 | $1, 207, 590, 862 |
| Public power districts_____ | 41 | 42, 448, 641 |
| Other public bodies_____ | 20 | 4, 776, 695 |
| Power companies_____ | 21 | 5, 119, 263 |
| Total_____ | 1, 034 | 1, 259, 935, 461 |
| Funds advanced (cumulative)_____ | | 877, 716, 224 |
| Amounts overdue more than 30 days: | | |
| Principal _____ | 69 | 480, 811 |
| Interest _____ | 69 | 596, 354 |
| Total_____ | 79 | 1, 077, 165 |
| Advance payments_____ | | 19, 239, 821 |

## DEFICIT

The financial report (Budget Treasury Form 30 Revised) indicates a deficit at March 31, 1948, in the amount of $11,369,093, comprising cumulative administrative expenses of $36,542,578, less an amount of $25,173,485 representing the accumulated excess of interest income over interest expense and provision for losses on loans.

Administrative expenses include certain expenses which, in effect, constitute a subsidy to the borrowers of REA funds. In connection with or in addition to its lending activities, REA provides legal, engineering, accounting, and other assistance to its borrowers, including assistance to sponsors seeking rural electric service to develop valid organizations, assistance to borrowers with respect to design and construction of facilities, installation of borrowers' accounting systems, advice and assistance as to all phases of management, etc., and in addition, conducts engineering studies and numerous other activities.

The 1948 appropriation for expenses of REA amounted to $5,000,-000, summarized as follows:

| Activity | Amount |
|---|---|
| Project development and allotment activities | $1, 037, 869 |
| Construction assistance to cooperatives | 1, 045, 829 |
| Technical operating assistance to cooperatives | 221, 840 |
| Management assistance to cooperatives | 762, 189 |
| Auditing, loan accounting and collecting | 1, 060, 019 |
| Technical standardization | 144, 150 |
| Internal administrative services: | |
| Property, administrative accounting, statistical mapping, and other office services | 300, 098 |
| Personnel services and stenographic pool | 130, 829 |
| Executive Management | 202, 022 |
| Information services | 95, 155 |
| Total | 5, 000, 000 |

The budget request for expenses of REA for 1949 is for precisely the same amounts, in total and in detail, as the 1948 appropriation.

Yours truly,

HASKINS & SELLS.

## Panama Railroad Company

SEPTEMBER 16, 1948.

HONORABLE HERBERT HOOVER,
  *Chairman, Commission on Organization of the*
  *Executive Branch of the Government,*
  *Washington, D. C.*

DEAR SIR: In accordance with your instructions, we have made a financial survey of the Panama Railroad Company for the period of 10 years ended June 30, 1947, for the purpose of assisting you in carrying out the purpose of Public Law 162, Eightieth Congress, under which your Commission was appointed.

Our survey has been based upon financial and other information available from official sources. We have regarded such information as reliable and have made no attempt to verify it through auditing procedures.

**126**

Moreover, we have not attempted to judge the efficiency of the management of the enterprise or the wisdom of the national policies in relation thereto as prescribed by the Congress.

We recommend:

1. That the practice of investing the Company's surplus funds in Government securities be terminated. At June 30, 1947, the Company's published financial report showed such investments to aggregate $19,330,000, which amount represented nearly 28 percent of the Company's total assets at that date.

2. That the Company's working capital funds in excess of normal requirements be paid into the United States Treasury in the form of dividends.

We summarize hereunder the more important facts revealed by our survey:

1. The Panama Railroad Company was acquired by the United States Government on May 7, 1904, as part of the transaction by which the net assets of the new Panama Canal Company (including 68,887 shares of Panama Railroad Company stock) were acquired. The authorized and issued capital stock consists of 70,000 shares which stands in the name of the Secretary of the Army, with the exception of 13 shares which are issued to directors.

2. The Company operates a railroad across the Isthmus of Panama, parallel to the Panama Canal, between terminal points of Panama on the Pacific side and Colon on the Atlantic side, a steamship service between New York and the Canal Zone, two hotels, and a number of other enterprises responsive to the needs of individuals residing in the Canal Zone, and to those of naval and other vessels passing through the Canal or otherwise utilizing its many facilities.

3. The operating policies of the Company are closely coordinated with those of the Panama Canal, and during the war years these activities were expanded and adjusted to meet Army and Navy requirements.

4. Since its early years when the Company received congressional appropriations, it has operated entirely with funds derived from its numerous enterprises. During the period from 1904 through June 30, 1947, dividends were declared and paid to the Government in the amount of $24,589,029. The most recent financial report published by the board of directors shows a surplus of $47,483,318 at June 30, 1947.

5. The Panama Railroad Company was incorporated by act of Congress approved June 29, 1948 (Public Law 808, 80th Cong.), pursuant to the requirements of section 304 (b) of the Government Corporation Control Act of 1945, succeeding the New York corporation of the same name.

**127**

The Company's accounts have been audited annually by independent public accountants from July 1, 1910, through June 30, 1944, when this function was undertaken by the Corporation Audits Division of the General Accounting Office. The General Accounting Office has stated that the accounts have been well-maintained and supervised and that, so far as it was able to observe, the Company has not entered into any financial transaction which, in its opinion, was without authority of law.

Our more detailed comments follow:

CREATION AND AUTHORITY

The original Panama Railroad Company, a private enterprise, was incorporated by an act of the legislature of the State of New York on April 7, 1849, for the purpose of:

* * * constructing and maintaining a railroad, with one or more tracks, and all convenient buildings, fixtures, machinery and appurtenances, across the Isthmus of Panama, in the Republic of New Granada, under the grant made by the said Republic to the said William H. Aspinwall, John L. Stephens, and Henry Chauncey, and of purchasing and navigating such steam or sailing vessels as may be proper and convenient to be used in connection with the said road.

A contract of concession directly between the Republic of New Granada and the Panama Railroad Company became effective on June 4, 1850; construction of the railroad was started in that year and completed in 1855.

The contract of 1850 with the Republic of New Granada was re-formed on August 16, 1867, by a new contract with the United States of Columbia, which had succeeded the Republic of New Granada, under which the Panama Railroad Company was granted, for a period of 99 years, the exclusive use and possession of the railroad, together with the buildings, warehouses, wharves, dockyards, and other dependencies necessary to the services and development of the enterprises then existing or which might thereafter be established.

The Company continued to operate the railroad under private control until 1881, when the first French Panama Canal Co. (Compagnie Universelle du Canal Inter-oceanique de Panama) acquired 68,887 shares of the capital stock, out of a total of 70,000 shares outstanding, by purchase from a group of stockholders. The first French Panama Canal Co. and its successor, the New Panama Canal Co. (Compagnie Nouvelle du Canal de Panama), continued to operate the railroad company as a common carrier, and also as an adjunct to their attempt to construct a canal, until May 7, 1904, when the net assets of the New Panama Canal Co., including the 68,887 shares of Panama Railroad Company stock, were purchased by the United States Government for the sum of $40,000,000 under authority of the act of Congress approved June 28, 1902 (32 Stat. 481). The remaining 1,113 shares of

Panama Railroad Company stock were purchased from the minority stockholders in 1905.

The concessionary contract of 1867, previously referred to, was materially affected by the convention of 1903 (Hay-Bunau Varilla treaty, signed November 18, 1903, proclaimed February 26, 1904, 33 Stat. 2234) in which the Republic of Panama granted to the United States all of the Republic's present and reversionary rights under the 1867 contract, together with perpetual railroad monopoly.

By Executive Order of May 9, 1904, the President directed that the policy of the Panama Railroad Company be harmonized with the policy of the Government by making it an adjunct to the construction of the Canal, while at the same time fulfilling its original purpose as a route of commercial traffic across the Isthmus. The Panama Canal Act, approved August 24, 1912, authorized the President to establish, maintain, and operate, through the Panama Railroad Company or otherwise, numerous types of business activities related to the Canal, and this legislation constitutes the basic statutory authority for the present activities of the Company.

MANAGEMENT

The authorized and issued capital stock of the Company, consisting of 70,000 shares with a par value of $7,000,000 stands in the name of the Secretary of the Army, with the exception of 13 shares which are issued to the directory for qualified purposes but which remain in the custody of the Secretary of the Army. The Secretary nominates or approves the 13 directors who comprise the board of directors of the Company.

From the time of its acquisition by the United States Government, the operating and management policies of the Panama Railroad Company at the Isthmus have been closely coordinated with those of the Canal. The Governor and the engineer of maintenance of the Panama Canal are president and second vice president, respectively, of the Company, and also members of its board of directors. Various other administrative and accounting functions common to the Railroad Company and the Canal are performed by departments of the latter, the costs thereof being apportioned on the basis of percentages developed through studies by the plans section, and the Canal is reimbursed by the Railroad Company for the latter's portion thereof.

At June 30, 1910, aggregate appropriations, including $7,000,000 for capital stock, amounted to $11,935,047 and no appropriations have been made by the Congress since that date. Thus, for many years, the Company has operated with its own funds on a "revolving fund" basis, and financial control by the Congress has been confined to limiting the amount of administrative expenses as presented in the budget.

Sources of revenue are the various operating functions, sales of investments or equipment, interest on investments, etc.

### Custody and Disposition of Funds

The Company's funds are deposited in private banks in New York City, and in branch banks in Panama. Depositaries are selected by the board of directors.

Funds are immediately available for expenditure upon presentation of properly certified and approved vouchers. No direct control over the Company is exercised by either the Bureau of the Budget or the Congress.

The Collector of the Panama Canal is agent of the Company for receiving the Company's funds in the Canal Zone and the Republic of Panama. Receipts not required for use on the Isthmus are forwarded to the Treasurer in New York.

A portion of the excess of its receipts over disbursements have been paid to the United States Treasury as dividends. Since the Government secured control of the Company's capital stock in 1904, and up to June 30, 1947, dividends have been declared and paid to the Government in the amount of $24,589,029. In addition, on December 16, 1943, for reasons of national policy having no relation to the business operations of the Company, the Company was required, pursuant to joint resolution of May 3, 1943 (Public Law 48, 78th Cong.), to convey to the Republic of Panama approximately two-thirds of the Company's lands in the city of Colon and practically all such lands in the city of Panama. The Company previously derived very substantial revenues from these lands which were carried at a book value of $4,666,979, but had been appraised several years previously by a board of independent appraisers designated by the Secretary of War at a fair value of $11,759,956. The Company's most recent financial report disclosed a surplus of $47,483,318.

### Operations

The operations of the Panama Railroad Company comprise eight distinct functions, as follows:

1. Railroad.
2. Harbor terminal facilities.
3. Coal plants.
4. Commissary Division.
5. Hotel Tivoli (Ancon).
6 Hotel Washington (Colon).
7. Telephone system.
8. New York office and steamship line.

The operations of the Company's real estate division, since November 1, 1944, are reported with the operations of the railroad.

Effective January 1, 1947, the operation of the Mindi dairy farm as a separate function of the Company was discontinued and the activity became one of the productive plants of the Commissary Division.

Following is a summary of the Company's operations (including interdepartmental transactions) for the year ended June 30, 1947, compiled from the annual report of the board of directors for that year:

|  | Total operating revenue | Total operating expenses | Net operating revenue (loss) |
|---|---|---|---|
| Railroad operations | $2, 708, 166 | $2, 415, 653 | $292, 513 |
| Harbor terminal operations | 2, 821, 982 | 2, 478, 722 | 343, 260 |
| Coal plants | 605, 236 | [1] 527, 863 | 77, 373 |
| Commissary | 32, 278, 463 | [2] 32,074,760 | 203, 703 |
| Hotel Tivoli | 636, 015 | 617, 779 | 18, 236 |
| Hotel Washington | 311, 188 | 317, 691 | (6, 503) |
| Telephone system | 370, 597 | 314, 571 | 56, 026 |
| Steamship line | 2, 438, 160 | 2, 264, 036 | 174, 124 |
| Total | 42, 169, 807 | 41, 011, 075 | 1, 158, 732 |

[1] Includes cost of sales, $262,210.
[2] Includes cost of sales, $27,414,335.

Net operating revenues as shown above do not reflect various additions to, and deductions from, income or surplus which resulted in a net credit to surplus for the year (after deducting a dividend of $1,250,000 paid to the Government) of $1,706,082.

The annual report for the year ended June 30, 1947, contains detailed information with respect to operations. This is not repeated in this report, but the following matters are noted as of general interest:

The Company maintained during the year total railroad trackage of approximately 162 miles (including Panama Railroad, Panama Canal, U. S. Army, and U. S. Navy tracks) ; it carried 616,249 passengers, 380,164 tons of revenue freight, and 6,349 tons of Company freight.

The Company's steamship line carried a total of 5,921 passengers of whom 5,192 were carried on Government account. The three ships of the line were restored to service prior to June 30, 1947, although reconversion and rehabilitation of the *Panama* and the *Cristobal* had not been completed at that date.

Sales of the Commissary were very largely to employees (76 percent) and Government activities, only 7 percent being shown as to individuals and companies and commercial ships.

The Hotel Tivoli, at Ancon, is owned by the Panama Canal but has been operated by the Company since 1929. The Hotel Washington, at Colon, is both owned and operated by the Company. The rentable room capacity of the Tivoli is rated at 132 and that of the Washington at 85. The facilities provided are comparable except that the Washington operates a swimming pool as a hotel activity.

Prior to the act of February 24, 1945 (59 Stat. 6), there was no provision of law which specifically required the Company to submit accounts to the General Accounting office. However, the accounts were audited annually by independent public accountants from July 1, 1910, through June 30, 1944. The first report on audit of the Company by the Corporation Audits Division of the General Accounting Office was for the years 1945 and 1946 and was presented to the House of Representatives on March 18, 1948, and referred to the Committee on Expenditures in the Executive Departments. This report is a very comprehensive one, consisting of 89 printed pages, and presents detailed exhibits and schedules relating to the financial condition of the Company as at June 30, 1944, 1945, and 1946, and its operations for the years ended June 30, 1945 and 1946. It comments that the accounts have been well maintained and supervised though recommending some expansion of certain auditing activities. It concludes as follows:

In our opinion, with the exceptions set forth below, the accompanying balance sheet (exhibit 1), the related income and surplus statements (exhibits 2 and 3), and the notes to financial statements (exhibit 4), present fairly the position of the Panama Railroad Company as at June 30, 1946 and 1945, and the results of its operations for the fiscal years ended at those dates, in conformity with generally accepted accounting principles applied on a basis consistent with that of the preceding years.

No provision for depreciation has ever been made on certain elements of railroad roadway and track (carried at a net book value of $1,091,361), the railroad signal system (carried at a net book value of $232,444), and the harbor terminals' moles, and roadway, walks, and fences (carried at book values of $337,479 and $56,781, respectively), which are classified by the Interstate Commerce Commission regulations as depreciable.

In addition to the elements of railroad roadway and track considered depreciable, as above, we believe that the remainder of the roadway and track account (carried at a book value of $7,085,159) is subject to economic obsolescence for which provision should be made in the accounts.

The dairy farm pastures (carried at a book value of $25,000) should be revalued by writing off a portion of such book value proportionate to the acreage abandoned and permitted to revert to bush.

The board of directors makes comprehensive annual reports containing statements of financial condition and results of operations and related statistics.

## Effects of Incorporation Pursuant to Government Corporation Control Act

Pursuant to section 304 (b) of the Government Corporation Control Act, approved December 6, 1945, the Canal Zone Code was amended by act of Congress approved June 29, 1948 (Public Law 808, 80th

Cong.), to incorporate the Panama Railroad Company. Unless dissolved by act of the Congress, the new Company is to have perpetual succession in its corporate name. The act provides, among other things, the following:

1. Transfer to the new Company of the assets and liabilities of the Panama Railroad Company (the New York company) as of July 1, 1948, to be evidenced by issuance of a receipt for $1 by the new Company to the United States.

2. The amount of the receipt to be subject to change by additional direct investments of the Government by repayments to the Treasury, and by other transactions described in the act.

3. The Company to be required to pay interest to the Treasury, at least annually, on the net direct investment of the Government as evidenced by the receipt described above at rates of interest determined by the Secretary of the Treasury as required to reimburse the Treasury for its cost.

4. The surplus of the Company to be defined as (*a*) undistributed net income prior to 1904, (*b*) the total net income from operations from and after 1904, (*c*) less payments to the Treasury as dividends from and after 1904, not applied as offsets to direct capital contributions, (*d*) less extraordinary losses or expenditures incurred through directives based on national policy and not related to the operation of the Company, not reimbursed through specific congressional appropriations, and not applied as offsets to direct capital contributions. The Company not to be required to pay interest to the Treasury on any part of its surplus, as thus defined.

5. Management of the Company to be vested in a board of directors having not less than 9 nor more than 13 members. The Governor of the Panama Canal to be a director and president of the Company.

6. On or before June 30, 1948, the New York Company to deposit with the Treasury the sum of $10,000,000 to establish an emergency fund from which the Company may borrow for any authorized purposes of the Company for limited periods only. The amount for deposit to be derived from the New York company's invested depreciation reserve funds and to be maintained by the Treasury as a separate fund. Loans from this fund to bear no interest.

Under the Government Corporation Control Act, the Company is required to submit before September 15 of each year to the President through the Bureau of the Budget, a business-type budget or plan of operations.

GENERAL

The Committee on Merchant Marine and Fisheries of the House of Representatives under date of July 2, 1947, adopted a report (Union Calendar No. 400) on the Panama Canal, its operations, and its future. This report set forth the findings of a group of members of that Committee who departed for the Canal Zone on March 27, 1947, in order to make first-hand investigations prior to introduction of contemplated legislation.

As bearing on the matter of relationships between Government and private business the following is quoted from the report:

Business enterprises operated by the Panama Canal and by the Panama Railroad embrace many activities which in the United States are normally carried on

**133**

by private enterprise. These activities have been developed to meet the needs of Canal employees and the needs of ships transiting the Canal. During the war years these activities were further expanded and adjusted to meet Army and Navy requirements. Business enterprises so conducted include the sale of food, clothing, and other essentials to Canal and Panamá Railroad employees, the maintenance of living quarters for such employees, the operation and management of the railroad and its affiliated passenger vessels, supplying fuel, provisions, and repairs to ships, and furnishing public-utility services.

* * * in addition to the operations of the Trans-Isthmian Railroad, the business enterprises conducted by the Panama Railroad Company include loading, unloading, storage, and transfer of cargo for shipping interests at the terminal ports; the operation of wholesale warehouses, retail stores, and subsidiary manufacturing plants engaged in supplying food, clothing, and other commodities to Canal agencies and to Government employees and their families; and the operation of coaling plants, hotels, a dairy, and a laundry.

These activities constitute "big business." The commissary division of the Panama Railroad is required to supply the normal products for day-to-day living purchased by all housewives. * * *

## The following is also quoted:

Members of the committee were much disturbed by the substantially greater number of Panama Canal and Panama Railroad employees employed today as compared to employment figures prior to the war. Comparison of prewar and present employment show that on July 8, 1938, the Panama Canal employed 2,942 "gold" employees and 7,683 "silver" employees, giving a total of 10,625. By January 25, 1947, this number had increased to 5,137 "gold" employees and 13,560 "silver" employees, giving a total of 18,697. Smiliar large increases are found on the rolls of the Panama Railroad Company which employed 442 "gold" and 3,945 "silver" employees on July 8, 1938, and 652 "gold" and 6,833 "silver" employees on January 25, 1947. * * *

Some reductions in force have been made during the past year. During the fiscal year 1946, the "gold" force was reduced by 767 employees, giving a reduction of 11.5 percent of the total "gold" force. During the same year there was a net decrease of 2,403 "silver" employees constituting a 9.9 decrease in the overall "silver" force as compared with the previous year. These decreases reflect the return of the Panama Canal activities to a normal operating basis following the end of active hostilities.

Your committee is of the opinion that further substantial reductions must be made in the Canal's force and made quickly. While decreases in the over-all force during the past year were made, your committee feels that more rapid strides toward reduction to a normal prewar complement must be accomplished. Unless prompt action can be taken by the Canal administration it will be necessary to recommend that appropriations be reduced to such an extent as to insure compulsory reduction in force.

Yours truly,

HASKINS & SELLS.

# Federal Prison Industries, Inc.

AUGUST 25, 1948.

HON. HERBERT HOOVER,
*Chairman, Commission on Organization of the*
*Executive Branch of the Government,*
*Washington, D. C.*

DEAR SIR: In accordance with your instructions, we have made a financial survey of Federal Prison Industries, Inc., from the date of its inception, January 1, 1935, to June 30, 1947, for the purpose of assisting you in carrying out the purposes of Public Law 162, Eightieth Congress, under which your Commission was appointed.

Our survey has been based upon financial and other information available from official sources. We have regarded such information as reliable and have made no attempt to verify it through auditing procedures.

Moreover, we have not attempted to judge the efficiency of the management of the enterprise or the wisdom of the national policies in relation thereto as prescribed by the Congress.

We summarize hereunder the more important facts revealed by our survey:

1. The corporation is not in competition with private industry.

2. While operations of the corporation have resulted in a profit in each year since inception, and while its selling prices are not in excess of current market prices for the same articles, it should be kept in mind that it pays no Federal, State, or local taxes and no rent, and that certain other costs and expenses for the benefit of the corporation (detailed later herein) are borne by other agencies.

3. The aggregate net earnings from January 1, 1935, to June 30, 1947, amounted to $20,074,871, from which $9,688,000 in dividends have been paid during the period into the United States Treasury. The corporation finances its activities from revenues derived from the prison industries and thus its operations are financed through a "revolving fund."

4. At June 30, 1947, the corporation was operating 43 shops, manufacturing 28 different types of products in 20 of its 27 institutions. Subsequent to that date production of mail sacks for the United States Post Office was begun at Atlanta, Ga., after a lapse of some 10 years. The total production was stated to be about 100,000 during the fiscal year ended June 30, 1948, and it is anticipated that production for the fiscal year ending June 30, 1949, will approximate 500,000 sacks.

5. The governing body of the corporation consists of a board of five directors who meet semiannually. They are appointed by and

hold office at the pleasure of the President, and serve without compensation.

6. Prior to June 28, 1946, the corporation had not paid any portion of its income as dividends into the United States Treasury, although accumulated net earnings reflected in earned surplus at the close of the preceding fiscal year on June 30, 1945, amounted to $17,399,042. Following a recommendation as to dividends (referred to in greater detail later) made by the General Accounting Office in the report on its first audit of the corporation (for the fiscal year ended June 30, 1945), dividends of $9,688,000 were paid into the United States Treasury during the two fiscal years ended June 30, 1946, and 1947. A further dividend of $2,000,000 was paid on January 28, 1948, and an additional dividend of $1,312,000 was authorized for subsequent payment by the board of directors.

7. Adequate reports are rendered in connection with the corporation's activities to the President of the United States, the Congress, the Secretary of the Treasury, and the Bureau of the Budget. Internal audits of prison industries are undertaken by field representatives of the General Accounting Office and the Washington, D. C., office of the corporation, respectively. An annual audit report covering the corporation's accounts is rendered by the General Accounting Office.

8. The General Accounting Office states, in its reports on audits for the fiscal years ended June 30, 1945, and 1946, that the accounts are well devised and maintained but that the internal audit staff should be increased.

9. Through all of the foregoing the Congress seems to be in a position to exercise adequate control with respect to the activities of the corporation.

Our more detailed comments follow:

ORGANIZATION AND PURPOSES

Federal Prison Industries, Inc., a wholly owned Government corporation, was created as a corporation of the District of Columbia by Executive Order 6917, dated December 11, 1934, issued under the authority conferred by the act of June 23, 1934 (48 Stat. 1211). It was the successor in corporate form to the operations theretofore conducted by the Attorney General through the Industries Division of the Bureau of Prisons as authorized by an act of May 27, 1930 (46 Stat. 391), which provided for the diversification of employment of Federal prisoners, and for their training and schooling in trades and occupations.

It should be noted that the authority of the Attorney General under the act of 1930 was limited and that he was not permitted to allow these industries to compete with private enterprise, as shown by the following language of section 3:

136

The Attorney General shall establish such industries as will produce articles and commodities for consumption in United States penal and correctional institutions or for sale to the departments and independent establishments of the Federal Government and not for sale to the public in competition with private enterprise * * *.

The act of 1934, under which the present corporation was created, contains the following provision in section 3:

It shall be the duty of the board of directors to diversify so far as practicable prison industrial operations and so operate the prison shops that no single private industry shall be forced to bear an undue burden of competition from the products of the prison workshops.

We are informed that no part of the articles produced by the corporation have ever been sold except to departments and independent establishments of the Federal Government (some of the articles and commodities produced are used in United States penal and correctional institutions, and sales of waste and scrap material and orchard and farm products are sold to private enterprise). Thus, it fairly can be stated that the corporation is not in competition with private enterprise.

Upon the Reorganization Plan II, part 1, section 3 (a), effective July 1, 1939, the corporation was transferred to the Department of Justice to be administered under the direction of the Attorney General.

## Business Operations

The selling prices of articles and commodities produced are fixed so as to provide a reasonable margin over costs, provided that such prices are not in excess of current market prices for the same articles. It is stated that the general policy of the corporation is to determine selling prices on the basis of considering its costs as 90 percent of selling price on sales to Federal penal and correctional institutions, and 85 percent of selling price for all other sales except those to private enterprises. The sales to private enterprises during the fiscal years 1946 and 1947 were of waste and scrap material and a major portion of the orchard and farm products at Columbia Camp (State of Washington).

The corporation enjoys the following advantages as compared with private industry:

1. It pays no Federal, State, or local taxes.

2. It pays no rent (except that, subsequent to June 30, 1947, the corporation will be called upon to pay rental for the separate premises occupied in Washington which heretofore have been paid for by some other agency).

3. Other costs and expenses not reflected in the accounts are reported by the Comptroller General in his report on the audit for the fiscal year ended June 30, 1946 to be the following:

    *a.* Cost of feeding, housing, clothing, and caring for the inmates employed in the industries is borne by the institutions and not by the corporation.

    *b.* Inmate labor employed on construction projects is not generally paid

**137**

wages, so that the cost of property additions and the annual provision for depreciation are both understated.

*c.* Certain services rendered by personnel on the pay roll of many prison institutions are not paid for by the corporation.

*d.* The services performed by the Division of Accounts and the Division of Personel of the Department of Justice are furnished without cost to the corporation.

*e.* Services of the Commissioner of Prison Industries, who is also Director of the Bureau of Prisons of the Department of Justice, and of the wardens are furnished without cost to the corporation.

*f.* The rates charged for utilities furnished to the corporation by prison institutions do not generally include a provision for depreciation of the capital assets which were originally acquired with appropriated funds.

*g.* The cost of maintaining the operations of certain industries which are regarded as more in the nature of a vocational training program expense, has not been treated as a direct charge against the revenues of such industries.

*h.* The Columbia Camp (State of Washington) orcharding industry has continuously been the recipient without cost of services, supplies, and use of equipment furnished by other departments of the Government.

On January 1, 1935, the Industries Division of the Bureau of Prisons transferred 22 industries located in 10 Federal institutions to the corporation. Since that date, the corporation has extended and diversified its operations by the establishment of new industries, the manufacture of a greater variety of products, and the undertaking of the construction of buildings and improvements needed in industrial and vocational training activities.

During 1935 the average number of prison inmates employed was 2,054, representing 15.2 percent of total prison population; for 1947 the number employed was 3,162, or 17.7 percent.

Wage rates paid to inmates during most of the fiscal year ended June 30, 1947, were 7, 10.5, 14, or 17 cents an hour, with time and one-half for time in excess of 40 hours a week, an increase of about 14 percent having become effective August 1, 1946. It is of interest that for the fiscal year ended June 30, 1946 (latest available), the cost of inmate labor was $601,931 representing 7.5 percent of total manufacturing or producing costs.

On June 30, 1947, the corporation was operating 43 shops, manufacturing 28 different types of products in 20 of the 27 institutions. The more important of these, as to value of sales, were canvas goods and textiles at Atlanta, brushes and shoes at Leavenworth, and metal furniture and clothing at Lewisburg.

CORPORATE MANAGEMENT

The governing body of the corporation is a board of directors appointed by the President of the United States who hold office at his pleasure and serve without compensation. It consists of five persons,

**138**

one of whom represents, respectively, industry, labor, agriculture, retailers and consumers, and the Attorney General. The board is required to make an annual report to the Congress on the conduct of the business of the corporation and on the condition of its funds.

The present board consists of the following:

Hon. SANFORD BATES, commissioner, Department of Institutions and Agencies, State of New Jersey (representing the Attorney General of the United States).

Dr. MARION L. BRITTAIN, president emeritus, Georgia School of Technology (representing industry).

Mr. SAM A. LEWISOHN, president, Adolph Lewisohn & Sons (representing retailers and consumers).

Mr. EMIL SCHRAM, president, New York Stock Exchange (representing agriculture).

Mr. GEORGE MEANY, secretary treasurer, American Federation of Labor (representing labor).

Mr. Robert J. Watt a member of the board representing labor, died on July 24, 1947, and the vacancy resulting from his death was filled by the appointment of Mr. George Meany under date of December 10, 1947, by the President.

The officers of the corporation consist of a president, a vice president, a commissioner of industries, and a secretary.

The president is the chief executive officer of the corporation and is a member of the board of directors. The appointment to that office is made by the board.

The vice president is appointed by the board of directors and is a member of the board.

The commissioner of industries is appointed by the president of the corporation and approved by the board of directors. He is the acting executive officer of the corporation.

The secretary is appointed by the president of the corporation and approved by the board of directors.

The present officers of the corporation are as follows:

Hon. SANFORD BATES, president.
Dr. MARION L. BRITTAIN, vice president.
Mr. JAMES V. BENNETT, commissioner of prison industries.
Mr. RALPH J. LAVALLEE, secretary.

In addition to the above officers specifically provided for in the bylaws of the corporation, Mr. A. H. Connor holds the office of associate commissioner and Mr. Jesse S. Barrows that of assistant commissioner, each by appointment of the board of directors.

The bylaws provide that all officers of the corporation not otherwise specifically mentioned in the bylaws shall be appointed or removed, and their compensation shall be fixed, by the Attorney General, on recommendation of the president of the corporation or the commissioner of prison industries, in accordance with the rules and regulations of the Civil Service Commission, the Classification Act of 1923, as

**139**

amended, and the other laws of the United States governing the appointment and removal of civil service personnel in the executive departments.

## MANAGEMENT AT FEDERAL PENAL AND CORRECTIONAL INSTITUTIONS

There are 27 Federal penal and correctional institutions throughout the United States. These institutions are managed by superintendents of industries, business managers, and wardens, respectively. At six of these institutions no industrial operations are performed.

## FINANCIAL

Pursuant to the provisions of section 4 of the act of June 23, 1934, and Executive Order 6917, dated December 11, 1934, the Secretary of the Treasury was directed to transfer to a fund to be known as the "prison industries fund" all balances standing to the credit of the prison industries working capital fund on the books of the Treasury. The corporation has no capital stock. Its original capital of $4,113,380 represented the depreciated cost of property, plant and equipment, and working capital of the Industries Division of the Bureau of Prisons, Department of Justice, as shown on the books of the Treasury at January 1, 1935. Intial capital has not changed since the inception of the corporation except for minor adjustments to reflect changes in the value at which assets and liabilities were transferred to the corporation.

Under the act of June 23, 1934, all moneys under the control of the corporation and any earnings that may accrue are to be deposited or covered into the Treasury of the United States to the credit of the prison industries fund, which is to be employed as operating capital for carrying out the purposes of the act of May 27, 1930. Thus, the corporate operations are financed from revenues derived from the industries without direct congressional appropriations. However, the annual Government corporation appropriation acts place limitations on the amount of corporate funds which may be expended for administrative expenses and vocational training expense. The corporation has no borrowing or lending power.

The net assets of the corporation at June 30, 1947, representing the investment of the United States Government, amounted to $15,000,799, all of which has been acquired through earnings from industrial operations. This amount is composed principally of net working capital of $10,869,919, and the net value of its plant and equipment of $4,166,182.

The operations of prison industries at the various institutions have resulted in a net profit in each year since the inception of the corporation on January 1, 1935, that for the fiscal year ended June 30, 1947, being $1,603,181. The aggregate net earnings of the corporation since that date to June 30, 1947, amounted to $20,074,871, from which two dividends, one for $4,774,707, and the other for $4,913,293 have been paid into the United States Treasury on June 28, 1946, and February 18, 1947, respectively. Thus, the balance in earned surplus at June 30, 1947, after deducting the dividends above referred to and net surplus adjustments of some $233,399 since the inception of the corporation, amounted to $10,153,472. This amount, together with the initial capital of the corporation of some $4,113,380, and its donated surplus balance of $733,947 (the latter representing substantially the value of sample cotton and wool secured from the Department of Agriculture) represented the investment of $15,000,799 of United States Government in the corporation at June 30, 1947.

The dividend of $4,774,707 just referred to, was stated to represent the value of all property turned over to the corporation at the time of its incorporation, $4,113,380, plus the value of property acquired from other Government agencies at less than market value since its inception to June 30, 1945, $661,327 (donated surplus). While it has been considered that the initial capital of the corporation was returned to the Treasury by the payment of this dividend, the corporation's balance sheet at June 30, 1947, still shows this initial capital, as the dividend was charged to earned surplus on its books.

In determining the earnings of the corporation, no amount is included as a charge against revenues for Federal, State, and local taxes which would be payable if the project were owned by private interests instead of by the Federal Government.

DIVIDENDS

Public Law 4, Seventy-ninth Congress, first session, approved February 24, 1945 (the George Act) and the Government Corporation Control Act (December 1945) require the Comptroller General to make a recommendation for the return of such Government capital or the payment of such dividends, as in his judgment, should be accomplished.

Under this requirement the report of the General Accounting Office dated May 1, 1946, on the audit of the corporation's accounts for the year ended June 30, 1945, recommended the payment to the Treasury of not less than $11,000,000, and the report for the year ended June 30, 1946, recommended the payment of dividends on the basis of each year's income after considering requirements for funds.

In addition to the payment of the two dividends previously referred to, which aggregated $9,688,000, a dividend of $2,000,000 was paid on January 28, 1948, and a dividend of $1,312,000 has been authorized by the Board of Directors. We were informed that the payment of the latter amount into the United States Treasury would be made during the month of August 1948.

Yours truly,

HASKINS & SELLS.

**141**

# Inland Waterways Corporation and Warrior River Terminal Company

SEPTEMBER 10, 1948.

HON. HERBERT HOOVER,
*Chairman, Commission on Organization of the
Executive Branch of the Government,
Washington, D. C.*

DEAR SIR: In accordance with your instructions, we have made a financial survey of the Inland Waterways Corporation and its wholly owned subsidiary, Warrior River Terminal Company, from the date of its incorporation, June 3, 1924, to June 30, 1947, for the purpose of assisting you in carrying out the purposes of Public Law 162, Eightieth Congress, under which your Commission was appointed.

Our survey has been based upon financial and other information available from official sources. We have regarded such information as reliable and have made no attempt to verify it through auditing procedures.

Moreover, we have not attempted to judge the efficiency of the management of the Corporation or the wisdom of the national policies in relation thereto as prescribed by the Congress.

We recommend that the Congress act on the recommendations already made by various individuals and committees, such as those contained in the audit report for the fiscal year ended June 30, 1946, prepared by the General Accounting Office, Corporation Audits Division, in the report of the Committee on Small Business in which it is recommended that the Government withdraw from the barge business, and the report of the Trundle Engineering Co., all of which reports are referred to later.

We summarize hereunder the more important facts revealed by our survey:

1. The Corporation performs services as a common carrier by operating barges and related facilities on the Mississippi River and some of its tributaries. Through the rail-switching facilities of its wholly owned subsidiary, Warrior River Terminal Company, its services are extended to the trunk-line railroads serving the Birmingham, Ala., district.

2. The operations of the Corporation and its subsidiary to June 30, 1947, have resulted in a consolidated deficit of $8,192,104, after transfer to capital of $97,913 received as a grant from the Federal Emergency Relief Administration on Federal works, and after making certain

adjustments for retroactive depreciation rate increases, and for the retirement of a number of obsolete barges and other floating equipment.

3. The Corporation has continued to operate with boats, barges, and other facilities acquired by transfer, at appraisal values as provided by section 2 of the act of June 3, 1924. After having served its useful purpose for about a quarter century, this equipment has become so obsolete that there is no longer any economic justification for keeping it in service. By prolonging the service of such obsolete equipment beyond its useful economic life, the management has been engaged in a constant struggle to keep the Corporation's activities functioning at the maximum level of efficiency attainable under the circumstances. At June 30, 1947, it appeared that the entire system must be completely rehabilitated at a cost estimated at $18,000,000.

4. The Corporation's records and those of its subsidiary have been audited annually by independent public accountants until the fiscal year 1946, when this function was assumed by the Corporation Audits Division of the General Accounting Office, in accordance with the requirements of section 5 of the act of February 24, 1945 (59 Stat. 6).

5. Various recommendations have been made to committees of the Congress but these have sometimes been conflicting and little definite action has been taken.

Our more detailed comments follow:

ORGANIZATION AND PURPOSE

The Inland Waterways Corporation, like numerous other Government corporations, evolved from action taken during a time of national crisis.

The Federal Control Act of March 21, 1918, as a war measure to relieve the Nation's overtaxed railroad facilities, authorized the Director General of Railroads to develop and operate transportation facilities on inland waterways. Under this authority, the Director General commandeered substantially all privately owned vessels on inland waterways and initiated a program of construction of new floating equipment.

By authority of the Transportation Act of 1920, the functions exercised by the Railroad Administration were transferred to the Secretary of War and operated as the Bureau of Inland and Coastwise Waterways Service. For the period from 1920 to 1924, the service was operated by the Secretary of War under the name of the Inland and Coastwise Waterways Service and was subject to annual appropriations for civil functions of the War Department.

The difficulties of operating under this type of control were soon recognized and resulted in the decision by Congress that under the corporate form of organization there would exist greater freedom from certain restrictions and the inland waterways transportation system could be more rapidly developed to carry out the purposes declared by Congress in the Transportation Act of 1920. Accordingly, by the act of Congress of June 3, 1924 (43 Stat. 360; 49 U. S. C. 151), Inland Waterways Corporation was created as a corporation in the District of Columbia. The Corporation operated under the direction of the Secretary of War until July 1, 1939, when its functions and obligations were transferred to the Department of Commerce under section 6 of Reorganization Plan II (53 Stat. 1434; 5 U. S. C., note to 133t).

The chief purpose and objective of the Inland Waterways Corporation is stated to be to demonstrate the feasibility of water transportation by operation of the Government-owned inland, canal, and coast-wise-waterways system to the point where the system can be transferred to private operation to the best advantage of the Government.

It was stated in recent hearings on the Government corporations appropriation bill for 1949 that the Corporation operates the most complete common carrier service by barge on the Mississippi, Missouri, Illinois, and Warrior Rivers. All types of freight, except livestock and perishables, are handled on 3,300 miles of inland rivers with 22 boats and 273 barges. Operations are conducted through numerous private terminals, as well as through 21 general merchandise facilities. Operations on the Ohio River were specifically excluded from enabling legislation supposedly on the theory that Government assistance in the development of navigation and related facilities on this stream was not necessary.

When the Corporation was formed in 1924, it was the expressed intent of the Congress that Government operation of this barge line should continue until the following conditions were met:

1. Until navigable channels have been completed in the rivers where the Corporation operates.

2. Until adequate terminal facilities have been provided.

3. Until joint rates with railroads have been published making joint rail-barge transportation generally available.

4. Until private capital engages, or is ready and willing to engage, in common-carrier service on these rivers.

FINANCIAL HISTORY

The act of June 3, 1924, authorized capital stock of the Corporation in the amount of $5,000,000 to be subscribed and paid for by the United States. This act was amended by the act of May 29, 1928 (45 Stat. 978), and provided for capital stock of $15,000,000. Appropriations of that total amount were made for the purchase of the capital stock but by an act of July 19, 1937 (50 Stat. 521), $3,000,000 thereof was repealed. The 1924 act further provided for the transfer to the Corporation of all assets acquired by the Secretary of War, or

144

which reverted to the United States under section 201 of the Transportation Act of 1920, as amended, at values adjusted and appraised by the Secretary of War at the time of transfer. The adjusted appraised value of the assets transferred amounted to $10,362,843, at which amount they were recorded on the books of the Corporation with an offsetting credit to Premium on capital stock account. This appraisal is stated to have been made by the American Appraisal Co. as of August 30, 1924, and to have been based upon cost of reproduction less accrued depreciation. The propriety of this appraisal has been questioned often and it has been asserted that the commercial value of the property at the time was possibly as little as $1,500,000.

In addition to the development of its original facilities the Corporation has since June 19, 1926, owned all capital stock of the Warrior River Terminal Company. That company was originally incorporated January 18, 1926, under the laws of the State of Alabama, as the Port of Birmingham Railway Co., with an authorized capital stock of $2,000. The authorized capital stock was increased to $150,000, and the company's name was changed to Warrior River Terminal Company, by amendments of its charter dated January 19 and February 12, 1926, respectively. It is reported that the purchase of the stock of this company by the Inland Waterways Corporation was made necessary by unsatisfactory interchange relations between Warrior River barge line operators and the railroad, to and from the Birmingham district.

At the time of its acquisition by Inland Waterways Corporation, $100,000 of the authorized capital stock of $150,000 had been paid in. By amendment of its charter the Company's capital stock was increased to $1,250,000 in 1931, all issued and purchased by the Inland Waterways Corporation. Additional funds were provided by a grant of $97,913 from the Federal Emergency Relief Administration on Federal works for replacement of trestles with steel spans.

The consolidated investment of the United States Government in Inland Waterways Corporation and its wholly owned subsidiary, Warrior River Terminal Company, at June 30, 1947, may be stated as follows:

Cash paid in for capital stock_____ $12,000,000
Assets transferred to the Corporation:
    Real property and equipment and miscellaneous
      supplies transferred from the War Department at
      appraisal values based on replacement cost____ $9,557,082
    Less: Excess of depreciated book value over esti-
      mated salvage value of certain obsolete floating
      equipment_____ 2,462,736
                                             7,094,346
Long-term loans receivable, less current liabilities, transferred from
    the War Department_____ 697,421

**145**

Appropriations made available to Inland and Coastwise Waterways Service_____ $108,340

Federal emergency relief funds allotted to Warrior River Terminal Company _____ 97,913

Total_____ 19,998,020

## MANAGEMENT

The Corporation is managed by the usual general officers, appointed by the Secretary of Commerce, who also selects the chairman and six members of an advisory board. The Corporation's bylaws provide that each of the six members of that board must be a recognized business leader in his community, shall represent one of the several sections of the country served by the Corporation, shall serve for 5 years, and shall receive no compensation other than per diem and travel.

## FINANCIAL AND ACCOUNTING CONTROL

From the time of its inception Inland Waterways Corporation and its wholly owned subsidiary were not subject to control through submission of annual budgets to the Congress until July 1, 1946, the effective date of the Government Corporation Control Act (59 Stat. 597) or to annual audit by the General Accounting Office until July 1, 1944, the effective date of section 5 of the George Act pertaining to audits of all Government corporations (59 Stat. 6).

The Corporation is not supported by annual appropriations from the Congress. Operations are conducted on a "revolving fund" basis. By this method the Corporation may continue to use funds provided as original capital and arising from operations. For the fiscal year 1947, for the first time, the administrative and general expenses of the Corporation and its subsidiary were limited in amount by the Government Corporation Appropriations Act, 1947 (60 Stat. 586), and for this same fiscal year the two corporations submitted their first annual budgets to the Congress.

The Corporation's records and those of its subsidiary have been audited annually by independent public accountants until the fiscal year 1946 when the audit was made by the Corporation Audits Division of the General Accounting office, in accordance with the requirements of section 5 of the act of February 24, 1945 (59 Stat. 6).

## OPERATIONS

At June 30, 1947, the Inland Waterways Corporation had been in the barge business for about 23 years. During that time, according to its published annual report for the fiscal year ended June 30, 1947, the operations of the Corporation and its wholly owned subsidiary resulted in a deficit of $8,094,191, which amount is increased to $8,192,104 by a transfer to capital of $97,913 received as a grant from

146

Federal relief funds. Of this amount approximately $3,904,947 resulted directly from operations before giving effect to the depreciation adjustments aggregating $4,228,255 described later in this report.

The Corporation's depreciation policy and its method of accounting for fixed assets in general have been vigorously attacked by its recently appointed president who stated in hearings on the Government corporations appropriation bill for 1949, "It is my belief that the equipment of the Inland Waterways Corporation has been carried on the books at an inflated value, and that depreciation rates used in the past have been too low." For many years the Corporation has depreciated its floating equipment consisting of boats and barges at a composite rate of 3.12 percent per annum. This rate, however, proved to be very inadequate as evidenced by the fact that the Corporation has found itself with boats and barges on hand whose useful life was ended but which the accounting records indicated to be only partly depreciated. The physical condition of the property with attendant high maintenance and repair costs has been cited as an important factor in the Corporation's operating deficits of recent years.

After consulting with the advisory board and the Interstate Commerce Commission (to whose regulation as to freight rates and accounting policies both the Corporation and its subsidiary are subject), the depreciation rates on the Corporation's floating equipment were adjusted retroactively to rates of 4 percent and 5 percent to reflect a proper service life of 25 years for towboats and 20 years for barges. These rates are in accordance with the general practice of the industry.

The adjustments of the property and related depreciation reserve accounts in accordance with the foregoing resulted in large charges to the Corporation's earned surplus (deficit) account represented by: (1) Retirement of 7 towboats and 2 tugboats which, after allowance for salvage, left $1,050,502 charged to surplus. This equipment was withdrawn from service and offered for sale. (2) Four other towboats, all over 25 years old, and 123 barges, all over 20 years old, were reduced to estimated salvage value leaving $2,559,111 to be charged to surplus. This equipment remains in service until it can be replaced with new equipment. (3) Depreciation on 4 towboats, 1 tugboat, and 94 barges, all less than 20 years old and still in active service, has been adjusted retroactively to rates of 4 percent on tugs and towboats, and 5 percent on barges. The resulting additional depreciation for prior years in the amount of $1,018,642 was charged to surplus at June 30, 1947, and credited to the reserve for depreciation.

The above major adjustments, aggregating $4,228,255 together with losses from operations (before adjustment) previously referred to of $3,904,947 account for all but $58,902 of the consolidated deficit of $8,192,104 at June 30, 1947.

At hearings on the Government corporations appropriation bill for 1948, Under Secretary of Commerce, William C. Foster, made the following statement with respect to the Corporation's floating and other assets:

In its earlier years the Inland Waterways Corporation developed the most modern and efficient towboats and barges in use at that time and established terminal facilities which were adequate for that period. In recent years it has not kept pace with the industry and as a result two-thirds of the motive power of the Corporation has had over 25 years' service, and the terminal facilities embody equally antiquated methods. The results are reflected in the losses of the Corporation and are such as to make it very unlikely that a private buyer will be found who will purchase the present properties of the Corporation on the terms required by the act; namely, with a guaranty that it will engage in a common carrier service substantially similar to the service now being rendered. On the other hand, continued operation on the present basis not only presents the possibility of continued losses but also the failure of the corporate mission of pioneering and developing river transportation.

In April 1948 a bill was introduced in the House of Representatives (H. R. 6236) to increase the capital stock of the Corporation to $33,000,000, and to extend the service of the Corporation to the Tennessee and Cumberland Rivers. The proposed increase is somewhat in excess of the estimated amount required to rehabilitate the system. No action was taken on this bill.

We are informed that during the fiscal year ended June 30, 1948, dissolution of the Corporation's wholly owned subsidiary, Warrior River Terminal Company, was authorized by the Secretary of Commerce accompanied by transfer of its assets to Inland Waterways Corporation.

Elsewhere in this report the expressed intention of the Congress with respect to the term of existence of the Corporation was stated as contemplating four conditions. These have occasioned much difference of opinion among various committees and individuals some of whom recommend the continued existence and rehabilitation of facilities of the system while others recommend its immediate disposal.

The report dated May 14, 1947, of the Committee on Small Business of the House of Representatives (Report No. 1102), contained findings and recommendations from which we quote in summary as follows:

1. The Government should get out of the barge business, and we are concerned only with recommending when and how that should be accomplished.

2. It appears desirable that the Warrior River unit should be sold as quickly as possible.

3. It is recommended that the Mississippi unit should be sold in a unit as a going concern.

4. We recommend that Congress approve rehabilitation of the Mississippi unit.

5. We recommend that the Corporation should continue its services on the Missouri River and should extend them as circumstances require.

6. It is suggested that the Mississippi unit should not be sold in sections.

7. Inland Waterways Corporation should proceed to offer the property for sale concurrently with rehabilitation.

8. It appears desirable that Congress should establish a commission of one Representative, a Senator, the President of Inland Waterways Corporation and a representative of the Interstate Commerce Commission to see to it that both the Mississippi unit and the Warrior unit are promptly sold.

9. It is recommended that the statutory prerequisites for sale or lease should be substantially modified by amendment of the act.

Each of the above recommendations is discussed in detail in the report which was fully approved by all but two of the Committee members. Approval of those two members was with the reservations that (1) the Warrior River unit should not immediately be sold because of congressional authorization of the Tombigbee waterway as a connection between the Tennessee River, Warrior River, and the Gulf of Mexico; they contend that resulting new river traffic should be pioneered by the Warrior River unit; (2) even before the Tombigbee waterway is built the Mississippi unit should operate on the Tennessee River.

Previously, in 1946, The Trundle Engineering Co., of Cleveland, Ohio, was employed to survey the records, equipment, facilities, and personnel of the Corporation and its subsidiary for the purpose of ascertaining the causes of continuing losses and obtaining recommendations designed to put the Corporation on a profitable operating basis. Portions of the Trundle report, which is dated April 24, 1946, are reproduced in the audit report of the General Accounting Office for the fiscal year ended June 30, 1945 (dated May 2, 1947—H. Doc. No. 234) together with notations by GAO as to certain corrective actions which have been taken.

Yours truly,

HASKINS & SELLS.

# Puerto Rico Reconstruction Administration

AUGUST 30, 1948.

Hon. HERBERT HOOVER,
*Chairman, Commission on Organization of the
Executive Branch of the Government,
Washington, D. C.*

DEAR SIR: In accordance with your instructions, we have made a financial survey of Puerto Rico Reconstruction Administration from the date of its inception, May 28, 1935, to June 30, 1947, for the purpose of assisting you in carrying out the purposes of Public Law 162, Eightieth Congress, under which your Commission was appointed.

Our survey has been based upon financial and other information available from official sources. We have regarded such information as reliable and have made no attempt to verify it through auditing procedures.

Moreover, we have not attempted to judge the efficiency of the management of the enterprise or the wisdom of the national policies in relation thereto as prescribed by the Congress.

We summarize hereunder the more important facts revealed by our survey:

1. A comprehensive report on a survey of Puerto Rico Reconstruction Administration, with recommendations as to its termination and liquidation, was made by Malcolm E. Pitts under date of May 15, 1947. Departmental recommendation for liquidation according to one of the plans proposed by Mr. Pitts was approved by Secretary J. A. Krug on July 3, 1947, and was later submitted for comment to the Secretary of Agriculture, the Housing and Home Finance Administrator, and the Bureau of the Budget. We are informed that their responses were unfavorable, and that no further steps toward liquidation have been taken. This plan was essentially as follows:

All individual, cooperative and hurricane loans, notes and mortgages on agricultural land sold, and grazing lands and bases would be transferred to the Farmers Home Administration.

All notes, mortgages and sales contracts, urban and rural housing programs (hoped to be 100 percent) and rental properties would be transferred to the Puerto Rico Housing Authority of the insular government subject to the review and general supervision of the Federal Public Housing Authority, who would act in the interests of the United States on all matters requiring Federal sanctions. PRHA would reinvest surplus receipts in new low-cost housing over a 49-year period.

Permit religious and other private groups to acquire properties to continue appropriate functions.

Transfer all other buildings and land to the insular government at no charge.

PRRA to act as disposal agency for all Government personal property not to be transferred as parts of * * * (the) above, which is over and above minimum administrative requirements.

Provision for a fiscal liquidation unit for 1 year after formal termination of operation activities.

2. Pureto Rico is essentially an agricultural country with a large population for its limited resources. In 1943 the density of population was stated to be 600 persons per square mile as compared with a little more than 100 per square mile in Cuba. The island produces slightly more than one-half of its food and devotes the best part of its land to production of sugar, tobacco, fruits, coffee, etc., for export, principally to the United States. Sugar has been, and still is, the determining factor in the island's economic situation.

3. The Puerto Rico Reconstruction Administration was created in May 1935, by Executive order of President Franklin D. Roosevelt following a visit to the island with his official family in 1934. The purposes of its creation are stated later herein, but may be summarized as the provision of relief and work relief and the increasing of employment within Puerto Rico.

4. For the period of approximately 12 years from its inception to June 30, 1947, expenditures of the Administration aggregated approximately $77,000,000. Its assets at the close of the period were about $18,000,000.

5. The Administration is currently financed by its own collections of interest, rents, etc. Its budget, which for 1949 amounts to about $800,000, is approved by the President rather than by the Congress.

6. Among the official reports or publications upon which we have necessarily relied are the following:

Rehabilitation in Puerto Rico—being an outline of the origins, of the functions, and the accomplishments of the Puerto Rico Reconstruction Administration. This is a profusely illustrated booklet published in 1939.

Federal Agencies Operating in Puerto Rico—is a report of about 250 pages prepared for the subcommittee of the Committee on Insular Affairs of the House of Representatives, Seventy-eight Congress, in connection with investigation of political, economic, and social conditions in Puerto Rico.

7. We have not visited Puerto Rico in connection with our survey and can add nothing consequential to the presentation made in the reports mentioned.

Certain more detailed comments are as follows:

ORGANIZATION AND PURPOSES

The Puerto Rico Reconstruction Administration was established as an agency within the United States Department of the Interior by Executive Order No. 7057, dated May 28, 1935, pursuant to the authority vested in the President under the Emergency Relief Appropriation Act of 1935, approved April 8, 1935, to initiate, formulate, administer and supervise a program of approved projects for providing relief and work relief and for increasing employment within Puerto Rico.

## BUSINESS OPERATIONS

The report to the Director, Division of Territories and Island Possessions, Department of the Interior, made under date of May 15, 1947, by Malcolm E. Pitts (to which reference has been made) states in substance as follows:

The operations of Puerto Rico Reconstruction Administration, since its establishment, have touched nearly every condition on the island of Puerto Rico that was substandard. At present its operations are confined to carrying on work already started from 1935 to 1942. During those years it was engaged in activities such as health, sanitation, urban and rural housing, demonstration farming, public works, work relief, development of sewer and water service, construction of highways, construction of hydroelectric plants and distribution lines, creation and maintenance of educational institutions, the development of home industry as well as heavy industry, loans to individual farmers and to cooperatives, and research in many economic, industrial, agricultural, health, and social fields.

The annual report of the Secretary of the Interior for the year ended June 30, 1945, includes a report by Benjamin W. Thoron, Administrator, which states that the main activities at that time had been curtailed due to the limited availability of funds. Hence, the comparatively small amounts which have been available to the Administration each year since 1942 out of the revolving fund have necessarily limited the agency's activities principally to the protection of investments previously made, and to conservation of the most essential features of its former broad program of rural rehabilitation.

The major activities of the Administration at the present time, on the basis of the Pitts report, may be stated as follows:

*a.* The operation and maintenance of five urban housing projects, and the collection of rents and purchase payments in connection therewith.

*b.* The management and maintenance of parcels of land in rural areas and the collection of rentals and purchase payments thereon.

*c.* The collection of notes receivable, which together with mortgages, are held by the agency in the name of the United States for land sold to farmers.

*d.* The management and collection of loans to cooperatives at various locations throughout the island.

*e.* The management and collection of loans to individual farmers.

*f.* The operation of Central Service Farms. This was a very important part of the original program, but at the present time only a few of these farms are in operation.

**152**

MANAGEMENT

The present administrative officers of the Administration are as follows:

JAMES P. DAVIS, Administrator.

E. BOYKIN HARTLEY, Special Assistant to Administrator.

GUILLERMO ESTEVES, Assistant Administrator.

EMLEN P. WAYNE, Chief, Finance Division.

HARLEY A. MILLER, Assistant General Counsel.

The Administrator of the Puerto Rico Reconstruction Administration, who is also the Director, Division of Territories and Island Possessions, Department of the Interior, was appointed by the President of the United States and serves as Administrator without additional compensation. The other officers, as listed above, are appointed by the Administrator.

At the present time the position of General Counsel is vacant, the former encumbent, Henry A. Hirshberg, having resigned May 31, 1948.

Under Executive Order No. 7493 dated November 14, 1936, the administrative acts of the Administrator were made subject to the control and supervision of the Secretary of the Interior.

FINANCIAL

The initial funds for the operation of the Administration were made available by allotments from appropriations contained in the Emergency Relief Appropriation Act of 1935 and later relief acts, and by direct appropriations through the fiscal year 1941.

Under the act of February 11, 1936 (49 Stat. 1135), the funds segregated or allocated for projects in Puerto Rico out of the money appropriated by the Emergency Relief Appropriation Act of 1935, were constituted a special fund which was made available for expenditure until June 30, 1940. All income derived from operations financed out of the special fund, and the proceeds of the disposition of property acquired therewith, were made a revolving fund available for expenditure for the purposes and in the manner authorized by the two acts until the Congress should provide otherwise.

This revolving fund, produced exclusively by operation of the Puerto Rico Reconstruction Administration projects, has been the sole source of the agency's financing in recent years, for no direct appropriations have been made by the Congress since that for the fiscal year 1941. Expenditures from the revolving fund, like those from the regular relief appropriations, have been on allocations by the President for projects approved by him.

Funds aggregating approximately $71,000,000 were made available to the Administration in the manner described through the fiscal year 1941. Since then, allotments by the President out of the revolving fund through the fiscal year ended June 30, 1947, amounted to about $6,700,000. Thus, the agency has received expenditure authorizations in the amount of approximately $77,700,000.

The aggregate expenditures of the Puerto Rico Reconstruction Administration for its entire period of operation to June 30, 1947, have approximated $77,000,000. During this period the agency has collected some $11,200,000, of which approximately $9,800,000 has been deposited in the revolving fund, and the remainder of some $1,400,000 (to March 31, 1947) covered into the United States Treasury as miscellaneous receipts.

The major expenditures represented in the total of $77,000,000 referred to are related to:

| | |
|---|---:|
| Rural rehabilitation | $36,606,000 |
| Rural electrification | 9,266,000 |
| Highways, roads, and streets | 2,366,000 |
| Rural and urban school construction | 1,935,000 |
| Forestation and reforestation | 3,410,000 |
| Urban housing | 3,228,000 |
| Construction of cement plant | 1,445,000 |
| University of Puerto Rico, including School of Tropical Medicine | 2,868,000 |
| Administration expenses | 5,810,000 |
| Total | 66,934,000 |

All other expenditures, aggregating approximately $9,900,000, accounted for the remainder of the total stated above.

The Federal Government's investment in the Puerto Rico Reconstruction Administration projects at the time of the Pitts report amounted to about $18,000,000 represented by the remaining assets of the Administration. These consist principally of urban and rural real estate, $7,800,000; loans to cooperatives and farmers, $3,500,000; notes receivable, $1,400,000; and cash of some $4,100,000, of which approximately $2,700,000 is available, from the revolving fund and about $1,400,000 is not available, having been deposited to miscellaneous receipts (as mentioned above) in the Treasury.

Yours truly,

HASKINS & SELLS.

# The Virgin Islands Company

Hon. HERBERT HOOVER,
*Chairman, Commission on Organization of the
Executive Branch of the Government,
Washington, D. C.*

DEAR SIR: In accordance with your instructions, we have made a financial survey of the Virgin Islands Company from the date of its inception, April 9, 1934, to June 30, 1947, for the purpose of assisting you in carrying out the purposes of Public Law 162, Eightieth Congress, under which your Commission was appointed.

Our survey has been based upon financial and other information available from official sources. We have regarded such information as reliable and have made no attempt to verify it through auditing procedures.

Moreover, we have not attempted to judge the efficiency of the management of the enterprise or the wisdom of the national policies in relation thereto as prescribed by the Congress.

We recommend further consideration by the Congress or appropriate committees thereof of the recommendations already made by various governmental officials and groups and quoted, in part, later in this report. We have not visited the Virgin Islands and can add nothing of importance to such recommendations.

We summarize hereunder the more important facts revealed by our survey:

1. The company operates in a sugar-molasses-rum economy which makes stable operation difficult. Nevertheless, from its inception to June 30, 1947, the deficit resulting from its operations (but without provision for rent or depreciation on properties operated under a lease agreement with the Department of the Interior and subject to other qualifications referred to later) was comparatively small, amounting to $118,752.

2. Considerable attention has been given by Government officials and others to the problems arising from the nature of the economy of the islands, climatic conditions, etc. A visit to the islands has recently been made by Members of the Congress and is the subject of a report referred to later. Reports and recommendations have also been made recently by the Senate Committee on Expenditures in the Executive Departments and by the General Accounting Office. The effort to

**155**

effectuate some of these recommendations through legislation by the Eightieth Congress, second session, was unsuccessful.

3. The accounts of the Company have not been well-maintained and have not been fully used for purposes of managerial control. Corrective measures have been initiated as set forth later.

Our more detailed comments follow:

The Virgin Islands were purchased for $25,000,000 from Denmark on August 4, 1916, to prevent their possible sale to Germany, shortly before the entry of the United States into the First World War. The Danes kept their interests in the docks, public utilities, and certain other businesses, while the United States acquired principally marginal land and assumed responsibility for the inhabitants.

The islands, which have a total area of 132 square miles, were under administration of the Navy Department until 1931 and since then have had a civil administration under the Department of the Interior.

In addition to the original investment of $25,000,000, the Government has expended approximately another $25,000,000 in the islands for Government administration, conduct of an experiment station, public works, and relief projects, including the cost of property leased to and funds invested in the Virgin Islands Company, established in 1934. However, it collected from 1934 through 1946, an estimated amount of nearly $56,000,000 as taxes on rum produced in the islands and imported into the United States.

In 1930 the Danish sugar companies, once very prosperous, collapsed and by 1934 the Government, through the Red Cross, was feeding 40 percent of the population.

In an attempt to furnish employment and thus to aid in some measure in the rehabilitation of the islands, the Virgin Islands Company was incorporated by local ordinance of the Colonial Council for St. Thomas and St. John, Virgin Islands (passed April 9, 1934) to function as an instrument of the Department of the Interior. The United States Government set up Federal Project 16 by the Public Works Administration, acting through the Department of the Interior. This project acquired the sugar mills, distillery, and miscellaneous properties from the defunct Danish companies, and an agreement, extended to November 26, 1949, which is in effect a lease agreement, was made with the Virgin Islands Company whereby the latter operates the properties, the rental consideration of which is the maintenance of the properties and the requirement to pay operating profits into the United States Treasury. The original cost of these properties to the Government (including later expenditures under Federal Projects Nos. 17 and 18) was $2,965,252.

No direct appropriations to the Company are made by Congress, except that for the fiscal year 1948 the Company was authorized to borrow $250,000 from the Treasury of the United States, and in the

156

1947 and 1948 annual budgets the Company was authorized to spend $20,000 of its funds in each of those years for administrative expenses, and in the 1949 budget to spend $97,880 for such expenses before apportionment of any part thereof to manufacturing or other expenses.

In connection with the increased amount in the 1949 budget, it is noted that the 1946 audit report issued by the General Accounting Office says with respect to the authorization of $20,000 for administrative expenses, "This amount was based upon only a portion of the Company's general and administrative expenses, inasmuch as approximately 70 percent of the total general and administrative expenses are customarily allocated by the Company to manufacturing costs; consequently, the amount of $20,000 is far short of the Company's actual expenditures for general and administrative expenses."

The Company has financed its operations through operating revenues, allocations made from relief appropriations, and borrowings from Federal agencies or from private banking institutions.

Capital stock, grants, and advances to June 30, 1947, less funds returned, were as follows:

| | |
|---|---:|
| 3 shares capital stock of $10 each, held in trust by a board of trustees for the benefit of the people of the Virgin Islands | $30 |
| Grants from Federal Emergency Relief Administration, Federal Security Administration, and other relief agencies, less funds returned | 899, 327 |
| Advances by Rural Electrification Administration, for which the Company issued notes payable of $209,302, and current and deferred interest on these notes | 226, 456 |
| Total | 1, 125, 813 |

The above grants from other agencies (less funds returned) to June 30, 1945 (total unchanged at June 30, 1947), were as follows:

| | Year | Amount |
|---|---|---:|
| Federal Emergency Relief Administration | 1934 | $200, 000 |
| Federal Surplus Relief Corporation | 1934 | 150, 000 |
| Emergency Relief Appropriation Act of Apr. 8, 1935 | 1936 | 168, 813 |
| Farm Security Administration—Rural Rehabilitation | 1938 | 230, 624 |
| Work Projects Administration—from Emergency Relief Appropriation Act of 1937 as supplemented by act approved Mar. 3, 1938 (Public Res. 80) | 1940 | 45, 331 |
| Federal Works Agency, Work Projects Administration | 1941 | 32, 181 |
| Do | 1942 | 52, 378 |
| Do | 1943 | 20, 000 |
| Total | | 899, 327 |

The Rural Electric Division, inaugurated in 1941, was financed by a loan from the Rural Electrification Administration on notes secured exclusively by a mortgage covering all assets, rights, and income of the system.

Below is a summary, by years, of the results of the Company's operations and sundry profit and loss adjustments:

| | Deficit [1] | Surplus [2] |
|---|---|---|
| General operations: | | |
| From inception to June 30, 1937 | $30, 504 | |
| Fiscal year ended June 30: | | |
| 1938 | 116, 636 | |
| 1939 | 9, 862 | |
| 1940 | 38, 297 | |
| 1941 | 60, 689 | |
| 1942 | 40, 988 | |
| 1943 | 23, 343 | |
| 1944 | | $413, 848 |
| 1945 | | 29, 881 |
| 1946 | 97, 776 | |
| 1947 | 85, 381 | |
| Total, June 30, 1947 | 503, 476 | [3] 443, 729 |
| Rural Electrification Division: | | |
| From establishment in 1941 to June 30, 1943 | | 535 |
| Year ended June 30: | | |
| 1944 | | 2, 701 |
| 1945 | 14, 203 | |
| 1946 | 27, 263 | |
| 1947 | 20, 775 | |
| Total | 62, 241 | 3, 236 |
| Net deficit, June 30, 1947 | 59, 005 | |

[1] Charged against grants.
[2] Reserved by corporate management for contingencies.
[3] Stated by the 1946 and 1947 audit reports to be subject to some inaccuracy.

In the foregoing figures no consideration has been given to depreciation of the Government property operated but not owned by the Company. A statement is made in the 1946 audit report that if such depreciation were given effect on the books the net operating deficit of the General Operations Division at June 30, 1946, would be increased by $1,310,193.

A further statement is made in the 1946 audit report that the depreciation provisions for the electric property are inadequate. The deficit of the Rural Electric Division is therefore understated.

Under the operating agreement with the Government, the annual net income of the General Operations Division (as distinguished from the Rural Electric Division) is payable into the United States Treasury unless temporarily reserved for contingencies. Net income of $443,729 (stated in the audit report to be not accurate) for the 2 years ended June 30, 1945, has been so reserved. Accounts receivable and inventories of rum, materials, and supplies, at June 30, 1947, aggregated approximately $833,000. Operating losses of the General Operations Division for the other years, total $503,476, have been considered as chargeable against relief funds. The balance remaining of such funds, $395,851, is considered to be invested in working capital and in land, structures, and equipment. These are in the nature of leasehold improvements, because, upon expiration of the operating agreement, they will revert to the Department of the Interior. The funds borrowed from the Rural Electrification Administration are invested in the electrification project.

Of the Government's original investment of $1,125,813, $1,007,061 remained at June 30, 1947, made up as follows:

Investment of U. S. Treasury:

| | |
|---|---:|
| 3 shares capital stock | $30 |
| Grants from Federal relief funds, less amounts returned and losses of $503,476 charged thereto | 395, 851 |
| Net income for the 2 years ended June 30, 1945, reserved for contingencies | 443, 729 |
| Total | 839, 610 |

Investment of Rural Electrification Administration:

| | | |
|---|---:|---:|
| Advances and current and deferred interest | $226, 456 | |
| Less operating deficit from electrification projects | 59, 005 | 167, 451 |
| Total | | 1, 007, 061 |

The three shares comprising the capital stock of the Company were held at June 30, 1946, by the Secretary of the Interior, the Under Secretary of the Interior, and the Governor of the Virgin Islands, as a board of trustees, under a trust agreement executed May 2, 1934, for the benefit of the people of the Virgin Islands.

The governing body of the Company consists of a board of directors of seven members, serving without compensation, elected by the board of trustees. One of the directors selected must be the Secretary of the Interior, the Assistant Secretary of the Interior, or the Governor of the Virgin Islands. At June 30, 1946, all three were members of the board.

Beginning with the year ended June 30, 1945, the Company's accounts have been audited by the General Accounting Office. The 1946 report states that the Company's accounts have been poorly maintained because of the difficulty of obtaining adequate accounting personnel and that as a result the accounts have not been used by the management for operating control as they should have been. In the past it appears that there have been frequent changes in personnel at all levels. For several months beginning in May 1947, the General Accounting Office assisted the Company in revising its accounting methods, but this work was suspended and information thereon submitted informally in October 1947.

From the beginning the principal activities of the Virgin Islands Company have been the production of sugar and the manufacture of rum from its byproduct, molasses. Because of the marginal character of sugar production in the islands, the Company has always lost money on its sugar production, but has in general been able to offset such losses by profits on rum.   The net income for the 2 years ended June 30, 1945, resulted from a temporary unusual demand for rum in the United States due to the whisky shortage.

A number of factors have combined to make sugar production in the island unprofitable.   Among these factors are marginal cane production caused by light rainfall, high evaporation, quick run-off, periodic drought, and occasional hurricanes; a tremendous increase in the world's sugarcane acreage; higher ocean freight rates than those enjoyed by Puerto Rico, which is the same distance from New York; and lighterage charges made necessary because ocean freighters cannot dock at St. Croix.   In the past several years all sugar has been sold to the Commodity Credit Corporation.   In the Government's 1949 budget the statement is made that in 1947 the sugar was sold at a loss of approximately $35 a ton.   On the other hand the sugar operation provides permanent employment for about 600 people during the cultivating and planting season and to a total of approximately twice that number during the harvesting and grinding season.   The distilling of rum, however, provides sporadic employment for only about 35 people.

Because of the severe drought and market conditions, 1947 is said to have been one of the worst years in the Company's existence.   Data inspected by us in the General Accounting Office indicate that the yield of sugarcane produced by the Company was 12 tons per acre in 1947 as compared with 17 tons in 1946, and that the yield in sugar was 174 pounds per ton of cane ground in 1947 compared with 211 pounds in 1946.   Under these conditions, despite the fact that higher prices were received for sugar, general operations resulted in a net loss for the year of $85,381.   This amount is approximately $30,000 greater than would have been shown if the Company had not changed its method of valuing molasses at the close of the year.   On the other hand, no provision for depreciation or rental, or other charge in lieu thereof, has been included in costs with respect to the property costing $2,965, 252 previously referred to.   It has been calculated that normal annual depreciation on all properties used by the Company would be approximately $112,000 more than the amount provided in the accounts and on a commercial basis the net loss for 1947, therefore, may be considered to be understated to that extent.

We understand that the 1948 crop is expected to be better than that of 1947 and that the sugar will be sold in the open market.

Under the Government Corporations Control Act of 1945, it was necessary that the Company be reincorporated under Federal law in order to continue in existence after June 30, 1948.   Legislation passed in June 1948 continued the Company as an agency of the United States until the close of business June 30, 1949, and authorized it to borrow from the United States Treasury such sums not exceeding

160

$950,000 in the aggregate as may be required for its operations to that date. Appropriation was made under the Government Corporations Appropriation Act (Public Law 860, 80th Cong.) of $500,000 for such borrowings and not to exceed $97,880 of the funds available to the Company were earmarked for administrative expenses before apportionment of any part of such expenses to manufacturing or other expenses. We are informed that the practical effect of the aforementioned legislation is to empower the Company to borrow an aggregate amount of $500,000.

An official inspection trip to the Virgin Islands was made during the period from December 26, 1947, to January 12, 1948, by a group headed by Senator Hugh Butler and Representative A. L. Miller and which included Mason Barr, chief, Caribbean Branch of the Division of Territories, Department of the Interior, and Mr. E. B. Van Horn, staff director of the Senate Committee on Expenditures in the Executive Departments. The report of Senator Butler and Representative Miller to the Public Lands Committees of the Senate and House of Representatives includes the following with respect to the Virgin Islands Company:

If permitted under the terms of its recharter, the Virgin Islands Company should make an investment in tourist development.

Legislation to be offered which will permit the Reconstruction Finance Corporation and the Virgin Islands Company to make small loans.

The insular government and the Virgin Islands Company to actively encourage the development of small industries after first obtaining assurances as to markets.

The insular government and the Virgin Islands Company to promate the growth and use of local products.

That the internal revenue tax on rum exported to the United States be returned to the islands in its entirety, but that this return be accompanied by restrictions as to the use to be made of the money.

That the Virgin Islands Company be given funds with which to make experiments in crop diversification.

That the Committees on Public Lands request the Appropriations Committees to give the Department of the Interior sufficient funds to repay the REA loan in its entirety and to operate the generating plant and distribution system as an integral part of the Virgin Islands Company.

That the Company be rechartered and that its powers and duties be changed and enlarged as recommended by the General Accounting Office and the Senate Committee on Expenditures in the Executive Departments.

Following are the recommendations of the General Accounting Office and the Senate Committee on Expenditures in the Executive Departments just referred to:

1. The United States Treasury should own the capital stock although the executive direction may continue to be in the Department of the Interior. The Treasury should be authorized by Congress to subscribe for stock to cover permanent requirements for both fixed and working capital.

**161**

2. The Company should be authorized to borrow funds from the United States Treasury for temporary working capital purposes.

3. The organic statute should provide, as in the case of the Commodity Credit Corporation, that the Treasury, subject to appropriation of funds therefor, shall be required to reimburse the Company annually for any operating losses. Similarly, the Company should be required, by law, to deposit annually into the Treasury any net income from operations.

4. Consideration should be given to the Company's owning all of the properties operated by it, including the rural electric project, although it may not have power to sell the properties except by superior approval. Depreciation on the property should be required to be provided in determining net operating income or loss.

5. The Company should not be required to make payments in lieu of property taxes and income taxes to the local municipal treasuries.

6. The proposed Federal charter should authorize enlargement of the activities of the Company and should provide for increased capitalization therefor. Enlargement of activities would result in the corporation's incurring expenses of a somewhat speculative nature such as those necessary to encourage research and experimentation, develop resources, enlist private investments, encourage and develop tourist trade, provide transportation facilities, and make loans for various other purposes.

7. Consideration should be given to obtaining insurance on the Company's property operated under the agreement with the Secretary of the Interior.

8. All employees having access to cash or checks should be bonded to protect the Company against loss or embezzlement.

9. In connection with the miscellaneous activities of the Company, it is recommended that the expenses or maintenance of employees' houses be subject to more control, and consideration be given to increasing the rental rates. The livestock program should be expanded or abandoned and consideration be given to leasing the St. Croix market and cold-storage plant to private operators.

10. The Company should take necessary action to recover title to 427.084 acres of land acquired by the War Department under Public Land Order 170 and 213.72 acres acquired by the same Department under Executive Order 8511.

The recommendations of the General Accounting Office and the Senate Committee on Expenditures in the Executive Departments referred to in the foregoing quotations are embodied, respectively, in the audit report for the fical year 1946 (referred to elsewhere herein) and in Senate Report No. 777 (80th Cong., 1st sess., Dec. 12, 1947).

H. R. 5904 (80th Cong., 2d sess.) was drafted to embody certain of the recommendations referred to herein and was accompanied by House Report No. 1699 of the Committee on Public Lands, April 8, 1948, recommending enactment. Before its eventual passage in June 1948, the bill had been so reduced in scope that only the provisions for the continuance of the Company to June 30, 1949, and authorization for it to borrow up to $950,000 from the United States Treasury, referred to previously herein, remained.

The subcommittee of the Committee on Appropriations of the House of Representatives in its consideration of the Government corporations appropriation bill for 1949 heard some 30 pages of testimony in April 1948, from Hon. William H. Hastie, Governor, Virgin Islands;

James P. Davis, director, Division of Territories and Possessions, Department of the Interior; Norman Olson, president, the Virgin Islands Company; and others, regarding the history and the various problems of the Company.

It is of interest that the opinion has been expressed by the Secretary of the Interior that the islands possess resources sufficient to make them self-supporting and the General Accounting Office has conceded the merit of the view. Furthermore, the chairman of the Committee on Public Lands in a report to the House of Representatives on April 8, 1948, said, "It is the opinion of the committee that the Company has contributed greatly to the economic life of the islands in spite of the shortcomings of the management."

It appears from the record that, in the aggregate, the history, difficulties, and problems of the Virgin Islands Company have been thoroughly presented to committees of the Congress, together with recommendations for future improvements.

Yours truly,

HASKINS & SELLS.

# V. CONSIDERATION OF THE USE OF REVOLVING FUNDS

## Methods By Which Funds are Provided for Expenditure

The Constitution of the United States provides (art. 1, sec. 9):

No money shall be drawn from the Treasury but in consequence of appropriations made by law * * *

Under this basic requirement there are a number of methods by which funds are furnished to governmental agencies and corporations for expenditure by them:

### 1. By Direct Appropriation

Direct appropriations may be (*a*) for a definite period of time—as a 1-year appropriation or (*b*) unlimited as to time—in which event the appropriation remains available until expended unless Congress subsequently rescinds the unexpended portion.

Direct appropriations, whether of the fiscal year or continuing kind, generally are made to particular organizational units for specified purposes. On occasions, however, funds are appropriated directly to the President in a lump sum, subject possibly to congressional limitations with regard to the maximum amounts which may be expended for certain purposes within the scope of the entire appropriation. Out of such a lump-sum appropriation, funds are allocated by the President, in accordance with the needs of the program, to various agencies.

The language customarily used in appropriation acts is "there is hereby appropriated out of any money in the Treasury not otherwise appropriated * * *"

### 2. Contracting Authority

A contracting authority permits the organization administering the program to enter into contracts, or otherwise obligate the Government for goods and services, in advance of appropriations to pay for them. This contracting authority must be granted by the Congress and is usually coupled with an initial appropriation. It follows that the necessary appropriations to liquidate contract authorizations are intended to be granted when required. An example of a program in which contract authorizations have been used is that for naval ship construction.

### 3. Guarantees by the Government

The Congress may authorize a Government agency or corporation to underwrite certain financial risks, such as the program of insured loans for veterans. As to that program, losses would be paid from appropriations made to the Veterans' Administration. There are other programs of guarantees or insurance, such as the insurance of crops by the Federal Crop Insurance Corporation, the insurance of home financing mortgages by the Federal Housing Administration, and the now extinct program of the War Damage Corporation, which was in effect during the late war to protect owners of private property. Losses under the programs of Government corporations ordinarily would be paid from the funds of such corporations rather than from direct appropriations. Expenditures to make good any guarantee or insurance, whether they relate to a program of a Government agency or a Government corporation, would not appear in the Federal budget until the money is required to be withdrawn from the Treasury for that purpose.

### 4. *Public-Debt Transactions*

The Congress may authorize expenditures by providing that they shall be treated as public-debt transactions, which means that the expenditures shall be made from proceeds realized from the issuance of public-debt securities. Depending upon the nature of the legislative authorization, these expenditures may be made directly by the Treasury without establishing a specific appropriation account on the books of the Treasury, or Government corporations and agencies may borrow funds from the Treasury with which to make the expenditures. Expenditures under such authorities are construed as withdrawals from the Treasury pursuant to appropriations. The effect on the level of the public debt, of expenditures under direct appropriations and expenditures handled as public-debt transactions, is the same. The public-debt transaction technique was first employed in 1932 in connection with borrowings from the Treasury by the Reconstruction Finance Corporation. The underlying theory was that the expenditures financed by such borrowings would be of a recoverable nature and that repayments would be used to retire public debt. However, the original concept has not been rigidly adhered to, since the Congress has used the device to authorize, in some instances, nonrecoverable expenditures by corporations. Borrowings from the Treasury by Government corporations are in the form of notes. Recent examples of the utilization of the public-debt transaction device are congressional authorizations for payments under the credit to the United Kingdom, payment of the United States subscriptions to the World Bank and Fund, payment for the capital stock of the Export-Import Bank, and authority for such Bank to borrow from the Treasury.

The foregoing are four basic methods by which funds are provided for expenditure. However, certain operations may be financed by methods which grow out of one of these four principal methods, such as (1) by reallocation of funds from the President's emergency fund; (2) by the transfer of the balance of appropriated funds of a predecessor agency; (3) by the transfer of capital or current assets from another agency without reimbursement, e. g., transfer of property by the Department of the Army to the Tennessee Valley Authority; and (4) by restoration of capital through cancellation of notes in favor of the Treasury, e. g., the cancellation of $921,000,000 of notes of Commodity Credit Corporation provided for by the Government Corporations Appropriation Act 1947 (appendix supplement, p. 66).

### DEFINITION AND EXAMPLES OF REVOLVING FUNDS

The following discussion of revolving funds is in broad terms and is not confined to the technical aspects of bookkeeping in the United States Treasury.

Unless a contrary provision is included in an appropriation, the maximum amount which may be spent is that specified in the appropriation and all receipts must be "covered into" the United States Treasury as "miscellaneous receipts" subject to further appropriation. An appropriation sometimes provides, however, that receipts shall be covered into the Treasury, not as miscellaneous receipts, but as repayments to such appropriation. Hence, through the realization of capital funds expended, the same fund may be used over and over again for the authorized purpose. Such an authorization may also provide for collections (of income) to be covered into the Treasury as repayments to the appropriation rather than as miscellaneous receipts. Appropriations which have these characteristics are technically described, in Federal Government parlance, as revolving funds.

Examples of revolving funds created by direct appropriation to agencies other than corporations are:

United States Maritime Commission.

Reclamation fund, Bureau of Reclamation, Department of the Interior.

Military and naval insurance, Veterans' Administration.

Agricultural Marketing Act revolving fund, Farm Credit Administration, Department of Agriculture.

Revolving fund for loans to Indians, Interior Department.

General supply fund, Bureau of Federal Supply, Treasury Department.

War housing insurance fund, Federal Housing Administration.

Fund for payment of Government losses in shipment, Treasury Department.

Vocational rehabilitation, Veterans' Administration, revolving fund.

The Merchant Marine Act, 1936, specifically designated a revolving fund, created from the funds of the "construction loan fund" together with the proceeds of various assets transferred to the Maritime Commission. The proceeds from the sale of capital assets as well as revenues of the fund were authorized to be used. Further appropriations by the Congress to replenish such fund were also authorized. This revolving fund was practically nullified by the Independent Offices Appropriation Act, 1948, approved July 30, 1947.

Numerous collections are deposited in the reclamation fund and out of this fund appropriations for construction, operating and maintenance, etc., are made annually by the Congress. Because of this action by Congress, the fund is not strictly a revolving fund. However, the Bonneville Power Administration has a continuing fund for emergency expenses of $500,000 and the Southwestern Power Administration of $100,000, which may be regarded as revolving funds.

As a general rule, Government corporations may be considered to be financed through revolving funds since their receipts are used to carry on the activities authorized in their charters, subject to the annual corporation acts passed by the Congress. It may be said that the excess of their receipts, if any, are for deposit to miscellaneous receipts in the Treasury (1) upon declaration of dividends by their boards of directors; (2) by specific action of the Congress; and (3) by dissolution of the corporation. Examples of revolving funds operated by corporations are as follows:

*Commodity Credit Corporation.*—The original capital of this corporation was $100,000,000 and it was authorized to borrow up to $4,750,000,000. Net payments made by the United States Treasury to restore capital impairment of the corporation, pursuant to law, amount to $1,964,000,000, consisting of $472,000,000 in appropriations and $1,563,000,000 of notes canceled, less $71,000,000 returned in the form of surplus.

*Tennessee Valley Authority.*—Section 26 of the TVA Act, as amended, provided for revolving funds but this was subsequently modified.

*Federal Crop Insurance Corporation.*—This corporation is financed partly by collection of insurance premiums.

*Inland Waterways Corporation, Federal Prison Industries, Inc., Panama Railroad Company, and Virgin Islands Company.*—These four corporations, apart from initial capital, financed their operations from their revenues.

## Types of Organization By Which Government Activities Are Carried On

There are two types of organization by which Government activities are carried on, as follows:

1. Executive departments, independent establishments, boards, and commissions, often referred to collectively as agencies.

2. Government corporations, most of which are wholly owned by the United States Government.

Generally speaking, the agency type of organization is concerned with normal administrative functions of government, usually involving expenditures of a nonrecoverable nature, whereas each Government corporation has been created for some special purpose, more often than not allied to a program involving recoverable outlays.

## Financing By Type of Organization

Government agencies are ordinarily financed by direct appropriations. Government corporations usually are financed initially with appropriations used to purchase their capital stock and thereafter with their borrowings and operating receipts. However, there have been exceptions in both types of organization and a few of them are noted here by way of example. Rural Electrification Administration and Farmers' Home Administration, both Government agencies, were given authority to borrow to obtain funds for lending purposes. As to the other type, Government corporations, a notable exception is the case of the Export-Import Bank, whose stock the Secretary of the Treasury was authorized to acquire from the proceeds of public-debt securities.

In both types of organization there are also found the other methods of financing mentioned, such as borrowing from the Treasury, using receipts from operations, reallocation of funds, etc.

**167**

## CONTROL OF APPROPRIATIONS AND EXPENDITURES

In Government agencies operating with direct appropriations, receipts and expenditures are controlled through warrants. Government corporations which are provided with capital and borrowing authority are not controlled by the warrant procedure, but operate almost exclusively through checking accounts with the Treasury of the United States.

All receipts and expenditures of agencies operating with direct appropriations, and the net transactions of wholly owned corporations exclusive of their borrowing transactions, are reflected in the Federal budget.

All direct appropriations and expenditures thereunder appear in both appropriation and expenditure columns in the tables of the budget document, and the Bureau of the Budget has included in the recent budget for the fiscal year 1949 estimated increases in outstanding borrowings from the Treasury as authorizations treated as public-debt transactions.

It has not been the practice of the Congress to include, in its accounting for the amount of appropriations made by sessions, authorizations to use the proceeds of public-debt obligations for specified expenditures.

## LEGISLATIVE STEPS

Congressional authorization is necessary for all of the procedures described above. In the case of direct appropriations, authorization is included in the basic legislation and a separate bill for the actual appropriation is handled through the appropriation committees of the Congress. In the case of public-debt transactions and other methods of financing, full authority is usually included in the basic legislation.

## BUDGETARY PROCEDURES

The normal procedures which must be followed in requesting and securing funds are set forth hereunder for (1) Government agencies and (2) Government corporations.

### 1. *Government Agencies*

*a.* Preparation of estimates, showing break-downs by objects of expenditure, such as travel, transportation, supplies, materials, etc., and as to personnel, by positions and classification grades.

*b.* Justification of estimates at hearings before the Bureau of the Budget as a basis for preparation of the President's budget, and later before the Appropriation Committee of the House and possibly that of the Senate as a basis for legislative action.

*c.* Conformance to personnel ceilings and other special requirements.

*d.* Apportionment of funds, for use in the current year according to periods of time, by the Bureau of the Budget.

## 2. *Government Corporations*

*a.* Preparation of a business-type budget program, including in the main, a statement of sources and application of funds, a statement of operations, with both actual and estimated figures, by major types of activities, and an estimate of capital or other funds to be returned to the Treasury during the course of the year.

*b.* Submission to Bureau of the Budget for review and incorporation in the President's budget and transmission to the Congress for approval.

*c.* Review by Congress as to its broad phases with such attention to details as the Congress may consider appropriate.

*d.* The appropriation committees of the Congress consider the annual budget programs of the corporations and report out a "Government corporation appropriation bill" which provides necessary appropriations and authorizes the corporations to use their corporate funds, within the limit of funds and borrowing authority available to them, to carry out their programs. (In past legislation the corporations have been required to restrict their operations to the types of programs set forth, but they have not been required to adhere rigidly to the amounts included in the various programs except insofar as the Congress has specifically limited expenditures for administrative expenses or otherwise. This gives the corporations considerable flexibility in carrying out their financial programs.)

*e.* There is no apportionment of funds by the Bureau of the Budget except that the Congress may limit each corporation as to the amount which it may spend for administrative purposes.

### Audit and Control of Funds

In the following paragraphs, there are summarized the various procedures under which funds authorized by Congress are controlled and audited, those applicable to Government agencies again being shown separately from those applicable to Government corporations:

## 1. *Government Agencies*

*a.* Amounts available for expenditure are established on the books of the Treasury in separate appropriation accounts.

*b.* Agencies requisition funds to be advanced to the credit of disbursing officers.

Both of the foregoing steps are accomplished through warrants issued by the Secretary of the Treasury and countersigned by the Comptroller General.

*c.* On the basis of vouchers prepared and certified by the administrative agencies, the disbursing officers receiving advances under the appropriations issue checks in payment of public creditors. These vouchers must specify the particular appropriations to be charged, and the disbursing officers must render formal accounts for audit and settlement by the Comptroller General specifying advances made to them and disbursements made by them according to each appropriation affected. The duties and responsibilities of the Comptroller General are provided for in the Budget and Accounting Act, 1921. In addition, it is the practice of the General Accounting Office to require delivery to it, for postaudit purposes, of the originals of contracts, copies of purchase orders, and other basic obligating documents. Also, there must be delivered to the General Accounting Office, under existing requirements, the originals of vouchers, canceled checks, depository statements, collection documents, and other evidence supporting the individual transactions in the disbursing officers' accounts.

Based upon this documentary evidence, the audit essentially consists of a scrutiny of the individual transactions to determine their validity under the related appropriation acts or other legislation, administrative regulations, and numerous decisions of the Comptroller General rendered with respect to specific types of transactions. The audit is also directed at the determination that appropriations, and legislative limitations sometimes fixed on expenditures within appropriations, have not been exceeded in amount, and that collecting and disbursing officers have properly discharged their accountability for funds which they receive and are required to disburse.

*d.* During the recent war, the General Accounting Office decentralized its audit with respect to cost-plus-a-fixed-fee contracts.

## 2. *Government Corporations.*

*a.* Capital or other funds supplied by direct appropriations of the Congress are established on the books of the Treasury in separate appropriation accounts (as in the case of unincorporated Government agencies).

*b.* Funds supplied by direct appropriation (e. g., for initial capital stock) and the proceeds of authorized borrowings from the Treasury usually are credited in full to the checking accounts of the corporations maintained with the Treasurer of the United States.

*c.* Since legislation applicable to corporations ordinarily does not require their receipts to be covered formally into the Treasury, such receipts are deposited for credit directly to the aforementioned checking accounts with the Treasurer of the United States. In a few cases, however, corporations are permitted to maintain certain funds in checking accounts with commercial banks.

*d.* The Government Corporation Control Act specified that "the financial transactions of wholly owned Government corporations shall be audited in accordance with the principles and procedures applicable to commercial corporate transactions * * *." Hence, the audit of Government corporations is made more along the lines of the business or commercial type of audit conducted by public accountants. Basically, the commercial type of audit is directed at determining (*a*) that the financial statements of the concern fairly present its financial condition and the results of its operations for the period under review in accordance with generally accepted accounting principles consistently followed from period to period, (*b*) that financial transactions have been conducted in accordance with duly constituted authority, and (*c*) that there has been adequate and faithful accounting for the assets of the concern. A further distinction in this type of audit is that the audits of the Government corporations are made at their places of business and such corporations are not required to relinquish their records or documents to the General Accounting Office.

The differences between the so-called governmental type of audit and the commercial type of audit are not so much in the detail and care with which the examination is made but rather in the underlying purpose and techniques employed. The former, being directed at individual accountability for the use of appropriated funds and the disposition of Government money received, might be considered as primarily a cash receipts and expenditure audit. The latter, on the other hand, is directed at the operations of the concern as a whole with, of course, due regard to a proper accounting for its assets and the authorized use of its funds.

## CONCLUSIONS AS TO REVOLVING FUNDS

Separate recommendations are being submitted herein with regard to the reclamation fund.

Revolving funds, both for Government corporations and nonincorporated forms of Government enterprises (exclusive of lending agencies) should be permitted under the following conditions:

1. Their use should be limited to working capital funds and the purposes for which they may be used should be clearly defined by the Congress.

2. Separate appropriations should be made for capital expenditures.

3. Working capital no longer required should be returned to the Treasury in reduction of the amount of the revolving fund.

4. Authority should be given for temporary borrowing from the Treasury, limited to a certain amount or a certain percentage of the working capital.

5. Interest should be paid into the Treasury as miscellaneous receipts on working capital (but not on supply or service funds) and on borrowings which the Congress has determined are repayable from revenue-producing operations.

6. Net income, after payment of interest as above, should be paid into the Treasury as miscellaneous receipts as soon as possible after the close of each month (net income being determined without formal closing of the accounts), so as to maintain the working capital fund at the amount appropriated by Congress. Deficits should be reported to the Treasury currently and to the Congress at least once a year for the purpose of obtaining appropriations to cover such deficits.

# VI. THE USE OF THE CORPORATE FORM FOR GOVERNMENT ENTERPRISES

### LIST OF GOVERNMENT-OWNED CORPORATIONS

At June 30, 1948, there were 75 active Government corporations including some with respect to which the Government's investment has been repaid.  While only a few of these corporations were surveyed by us, we were able to ascertain that all of them had revolving funds.  The list of active corporations is as follows:

Farm Credit Administration group:
    Banks for Cooperatives:
        Central Bank _____ 1
        District Banks_____ 12
    Federal Farm Mortgage Corporation_____ 1
    Federal Intermediate Credit Banks_____ 12
    Federal Land Banks_____ 12
    Production Credit Corporations_____ 12
    Regional Agricultural Credit Corporation_____ 1
                                                    — 51

Reconstruction Finance Corporation group:
    Federal National Mortgage Association_____ 1
    Reconstruction Finance Corporation_____ 1
                                                    — 2

Housing and Home Finance group:
    Federal Home Loan Banks_____ 11
Federal Public Housing Authority (or U. S. Housing Authority),
    now Public Housing Administration_____ 1
    Federal Savings and Loan Insurance Corporation_____ 1
                                                   — 13

Production and Marketing group:
    Commodity Credit Corporation_____ 1
    Federal Crop Insurance Corporation_____ 1
                                                   — 2

Inland Waterways Corporation_____ 1
Export-Import Bank of Washington (federally reincorporated by Public
    Law 89, June 9, 1947)_____ 1
Federal Deposit Insurance Corporation_____ 1
Federal Prison Industries, Inc_____ 1
Panama Railroad Company_____ 1
Tennessee Valley Authority_____ 1
Virgin Islands Company_____ 1

    Total_____ 75

172

NOTE.—Since the date of the Government Corporation Control Act, December 6, 1945, 11 corporations have been completely dissolved; 3 have been eliminated by merger; 1 corporation, Farmers Home Corporation, has never been in operation.

In addition to the foregoing, there were 12 corporations in process of liquidation at June 30, 1948, as follows:

Home Loan Bank Board:
 Home Owners' Loan Corporation_____ 1
Inter-American Affairs group:
 The Institute of Inter-American Affairs (b) (d) _____ 1
 Institute of Inter-American Transportation (d) _____ 1
 Inter-American Educational Foundation, Inc. (b) (d) _____ 1
 Prencinradio, Inc. (d) _____ 1
                     — 4

Public Housing Administration:
 Defense Homes Corporation_____ 1
Reconstruction Finance Corporation group:
 The RFC Mortgage Company (a) (e) _____ 1
 Rubber Development Corporation (a) (d) _____ 1
 U. S. Commercial Company (f) _____ 1
 War Damage Corporation_____ 1
                     — 4
Tennessee Valley Associated Cooperatives, Inc_____ 1
U. S. Housing Corporation (c) _____ 1

 Total_____ 12

*Legend:*

 *a.* Transferred to Reconstruction Finance Corporation.

 *b.* Transferred to the Institute of Inter-American Affairs, a Federal corporation created by Public Law 369, August 5, 1947.

 *c.* Legal dissolution delayed due to lack of funds—all moneys having been returned to the Treasury—authority requested by the Bureau of the Budget to permit Home Owners' Loan Corporation to pay such expenses estimated at $5,000—minor claims concluded (S. Doc. 163, 80th Cong.).

 *d.* Delaware law requires corporate existence for at least 3 years after the filing of certificate of dissolution.

 *e.* Maryland charter not yet dissolved.

 *f.* Pursuant to Public Law 132, Eightieth Congress, succession of the corporation was extended only to June 30, 1948.

## ADVANTAGES AND DISADVANTAGES OF CORPORATE FORM

The Government enterprise in noncorporate form has certain disadvantages from an operating point of view. Because of the lack of flexibility in its budget and because, as with Government corporations, it has to estimate its requirements for the ensuing fiscal year almost 2 years before the time when the last of the appropriation will be spent, any new project which becomes necessary and for which no appropriation was made, could only be provided for by a contract embodying a condition that the funds be appropriated by the Congress. It cannot sue and be sued like a Government corporation and is thereby at a disadvantage in dealing with the public.

In the corporate form, the accounts may be kept on a basis which segregates expenses by character or activity, thus providing a type of report which is required by management for efficient operation and furnishing the information necessary for the business-type budget authorized for use by corporations under the Government Corporation Control Act. In noncorporate enterprises, the budget must be prepared from accounts kept on the customary appropriation basis by object of expenditure. If published reports of such enterprises are prepared on the corporate basis, complicated reconcilements are necessary to explain the differences between such reports and repayment and budget reports prepared on the appropriation basis.

The disadvantages which have been imputed to the use of the corporate form are largely due to abuses arising from lack of adequate control by the Government. There seems to be a belief that Government corporations have tended to become too independent and have failed to cooperate properly with other agencies of the Government. These disadvantages should largely disappear if administration is by qualified boards of directors concerned only with policy making, properly prepared business-type reports and business-type audits are made, and it is required that revenues be available only for current operating costs, all expenditures for plant expansion and non-revenue-producing programs being made from appropriations therefor.

## WHEN RECOMMENDED

The corporate form is recommended only for those enterprises which meet the following requirements:

*a.* The operations should be predominantly of a business nature, involving business-type transactions with the public or with private industry.

*b.* At least the major programs should be revenue producing.

Obviously, such operations are not susceptible of the accurate forecasting required for the preparation of the customary appropriation-type budget and therefore the corporate form with its more flexible business-type budget offers substantial advantages.

The President's message to the Congress of January 3, 1947, transmitting the budget for the fiscal year 1948 included the following with respect to Government corporations:

> While the general role of the Government corporation has been accepted in the laws of this country for more than 30 years, the standards for use of this instrument are not fully developed and will be subject to many refinements. Experience indicates that the corporate form of organization is peculiarly adapted to the administration of governmental programs which are predominantly of a commercial character—those which are revenue producing, are at least potentially

self-sustaining, and involve a large number of business-type transactions with the public.

In their business operations such programs require greater flexibility than the customary type of appropriation budget ordinarily permits. As a rule the usefulness of a corporation lies in its ability to deal with the public in the manner employed by private business for similar work. Necessary controls are or can be provided under the Government Corporation Control Act. Further study may well indicate not only that some existing corporations ought to be converted into agencies, but also that some existing agencies might administer their programs more effectively if they had some or all of the attributes of corporations.

## MANAGEMENT

The management of each Government corporation should be vested in a small board of directors, on a part-time basis, who would be responsible, within the limits of authority prescribed by the Congress, for policy making, including approval of business-type budgets in a condensed form. No administrative functions would be performed by the board. The board would report to the Congress through the President. The objection to full-time boards of directors is that they do not limit themselves to policy matters, but participate actively in corporation administration and that they tend to intensify the problem of exclusive autonomy of corporations. In cases where the corporation is an integral part of a regular agency, the chairman of the board may be the head of the agency with a subordinate agency staff comprising the balance of the board. Such a board may become in effect a rubber-stamp board, and thus a device to subordinate the corporation to the agency. The formation of a board of directors consisting of heads or representatives of interested agencies is a device to achieve interagency coordination, which probably could be better accomplished by interagency coordinating committees. Provision should be made for a comptroller capable of achieving the requisite cooperation with management at the top level and of giving adequate supervision to the accounts.

The requirement of a business-type audit of Government corporations will result in simpler and more standardized reports on the operations of these agencies than those presently available. Similarly, simplified and standardized requirements could be set up for the preparation of budgets and repayment reports. For example, in the repayment reports of various power projects, much of the voluminous, confusing detail, the unclear presentations, and the variations in form which are now present, could be eliminated to the end that the performance of the various projects could be equitably compared.

## LEGAL FORM OF GOVERNMENT'S INVESTMENT

It has usually been the practice to finance Government corporations initially through the issuance of capital stock to the Treasury Department. Apart from some possible legal requirement for a nominal amount of capital stock, there seems to be no good reason for the practice. Instead, appropriations by the Congress to finance the corporation should take the form of advances from the Treasury, appropriations and advances for construction to be kept separately, as recommended elsewhere herein, from appropriations and advances for working capital. As stated in our recommendations, all appropriations which the Congress may determine to be repayable from revenue-producing operations should bear interest at a rate to be fixed by the Secretary of the Treasury.

A draft of a proposed form of charter for Government corporations has been prepared by John E. Masten and has been submitted to your Commission. This draft contains certain provisions with respect to taxes or other payments in lieu thereof. We consider this matter to be one involving questions of national policy, which, as previously stated, we regard as beyond the sphere of our special qualifications as accountants. It also contains provisions for giving to the Treasury Department notes for all advances for capital and working funds. While it seems to us that this is a step which would serve no essential accounting purpose and would place some procedural burdens on those concerned, it would no doubt facilitate the carrying out of the will of the Congress in cases where repayment of amounts expended pursuant to appropriation is required.